HOOK 'EM HORNS

A Story of Texas Football

HOOK 'EM HORNS

A Story of Texas Football

by
Denne H. Freeman

THE STRODE PUBLISHERS
HUNTSVILLE, ALABAMA 35802

Copyright 1974
By Denne H. Freeman
All Rights In This Book
Reserved Including The Right
To Reproduce This Book Or Parts
Thereof In Any Form — Printed In U.S.A.
Library Of Congress Catalog Number 74-84329
Standard Book Number 87397-054-3

To My Wife, Mary, The
Children, And My Parents,
With Love

To All Longhorn Fans:
"Hook 'Em."

All Photographs Courtesy Of
University of Texas, Southwest
Conference, Cotton Bowl Athletic
Association, and Linda Kaye

Contents

Foreword
1. The Big Games 11
2. From The State Title To The Big Top 19
3. Clyde Littlefield 30
4. 1934-1936 And A Stroke Of Glory 36
5. How It Was 39
6. The Leather Helmet Era 41
7. Dana Xeonophon Bible 46
8. The All-American Water Boy And
   Friend Bobby 62
9. The Mission Kid 67
10. The Blond Bomber 71

11.	Company Men	77
12.	The Royal Reign	85
13.	Getting Navy's Goat	93
14.	Leaves In The Wind	98
15.	Coach Campbell	104
16.	Big Red	109
17.	Royal And Recruiting	112
18.	The Birth Of The Wishbone	116
19.	Once In A Lifetime	122
20.	The Fourth Down Phantom	128
21.	A Game Ball For Freddie	134
22.	Symbol Of Courage	138
23.	Scribes And The Man	143
24.	Orange Infusion	148
25.	The Minority Stigma	156
26.	The Sledgehammer	160
27.	DKR And Hanging Out	164
28.	Home Sweet Home	170
29.	World's Tallest Fat Man	176
30.	Royalisms	182
	Appendix	189

Foreword

"HOOK 'EM HORNS" originated as a University of Texas battle cry at a football pep rally in 1955. It means simply give 100 percent on the field and you can hold your head high in both victory and defeat. We try our darndest to keep from experiencing the latter.

Author Denne Freeman shows you in this story on UT football that there's more to it than just lining up and kicking it off every Saturday. There's a tremendous amount of hard work, dedication, and the ever present recruiting pressure that goes into Saturday's product.

I think you will find a lot to interest and entertain you between the covers of Freeman's book.

"Hook 'Em Horns!"

Darrell Royal
University of Texas

The Big Games

The University f Texas has played more than its share of pressure-cooker   s from 1893 to 1974, and the hard-earned victories provi   any late evening topics at any gathering of the Longhorn   . For some, the Longhorns' 18-16 win over Dallas in the fi   appearance of a 'Horn football team is no less important than 1969s Shootout I beating of Arkansas for the national title.

Wilbur Evans, an administrator with the Cotton Bowl Athletic Association and Southwest Conference, remembers farther back than most. A 1935 Texas grad, he began chronicling the Longhorns in 1931 as a writer for the school newspaper, the Daily Texan, *then later was sports information director at Austin for twelve years.*

Once asked to log the major victories by the winningest football school in the Southwest, Evans labored over the project for days. He of course starts with the 1969 win over Arkansas in Fayetteville—a 15-14 goose pimpler in which the Longhorns erased a 14-0 deficit late in the game. He follows that with the 1970 Cotton Bowl when Texas handed Notre Dame a 21-17 defeat that erased any doubts whether Texas deserved laurels as the nation's top team.

Those picks were the easy ones. But Evans found others:

To George Fitts, said Evans, Texas' most significant triumph was the 1958 conquest of Texas A&M to restore the Longhorns' domination of the Aggies in Memorial Stadium. To Fitts, the game was especially notable because it was his only appearance in an Orange and White uniform.

Captain James Morrison and his teammates savored a Thanksgiving Day, 1893, win at Dallas because the 18-16 conquest of Dallas at the Fairgrounds was the first game ever for a Texas football team, and the inaugural season was not marred by defeat in five games.

Darrell Royal's 1963 Longhorns became the first of three Texas teams to attain national championship success. The other two kings were the 1969 and 1970 squads.

The 1963 club scored such significant conquests as a 7-0 defeat of Baylor, an incredible come-from-behind decision over Texas A&M, and a 28-7 thrashing of Oklahoma, the nation's top-ranked team going into the contest with the Longhorns.

Among the most significant of all Texas victories was the 1963 club's New Year's Day, 1964, triumph over Navy in the Cotton Bowl, matching the nation's No. 1 ranked eleven, Texas, against the runnerup. As the players were introduced, Navy coach Wayne Hardin pleaded over the public address system and national television: "If the challenger should beat the champion, the challenger should be the champion."

Phil Harris of the Longhorns, who caught two touchdown bombs in the game, said, "We backs were standing behind our linemen and could see their necks turning red as he (Hardin) made that challenge."

An aroused, stubborn defense figured strongly in Texas' subsequent 28-6 victory in which Navy was held to minus yardage rushing, and a balanced offensive attack spotlighting Harris and quarterback Duke Carlisle rolled through the Middies.

In 1964 a 14-13 loss to Arkansas came when Texas failed on a two-point conversion attempt that could have meant victory, but the Longhorns were still invited to the Orange Bowl to meet an Alabama team that was designated by the Associated Press as national champion. Fifth-ranked Texas, using a 79-yard gallop by Ernie Koy and a 69-yard pass play from Jim Hudson to George Sauer, had built a 21-7 lead over the Crimson Tide at half time.

Even then a late-game goal line stand was needed to preserve a 21-17 victory. Joe Namath, who sparked an Alabama comeback, was stopped on fourth down from the two-yard line by Tommy Nobis, Clayton Lacy, Diron Talbert, and Olen Underwood.

Texas of 1972 upset another highly-rated Alabama team to keep clean Royal's mark of having never lost to a team coached by Bear Bryant, the one-time Texas A&M coach who is revered in Texas as one of the greatest in the game. That came in the Cotton Bowl 17-13.

Four decades earlier Texas and Rice boosted the Southwest Conference into national recognition when the Longhorns shocked Notre Dame 7-6 and Rice tripped up Purdue on the same Saturday in 1934. It was the Irish's first opening day loss ever.

All the scoring came in the first 57 seconds of the 1940 A&M-Texas game, but drama hung over the field until the final gun.

"The game marked one of the few times in my coaching career that our team was afforded an opportunity to employ a play that we had rehearsed for a specific situation," said former coach Dana X. Bible.

Using Jack Crain at fullback instead of tailback, Pete Layden connected with a 32-yard pass on the first play, setting up Layden's eventual one-yard sneak for what proved the winning touchdown against the surprised Aggies. The 7-0 upset, achieved by a group of players who became known as the immortal 13, ended an A&M winning streak of 19 games and denied the Aggies a possible second straight national championship and a certain bid to the Rose Bowl.

A rebirth of football prosperity came to Texas in 1939 when those 1941 seniors were sophomores. A single minute of play changed defeat into victory and turned the attitude at the Forty Acres from losing to winning.

It was the final minute of play against Arkansas on October 21, 1939. The Razorbacks were the apparent victors, leading 13-7 with Texas in possession at its own thirty-one. The second hand was making its final sweep as fans moved toward the exit.

Johnny Gill called an ordinary flat-zone pass, but switched his blocking back assignment with Crain. The ball was snapped to R. B. Patrick who flipped a short pass to Crain in the right flat, and Cowboy Jack began a dazzling trip that carried 69 yards for a touchdown that tied the score. When Crain kicked the extra point for a 14-13 win, Texas backers went wild. Twice the mob swarmed over the playing field delaying the final seconds of play for a kickoff, postponing a threatening but futile attempt by Arkansas to fight back.

Texas' first Southwest Conference championship was claimed on Thanksgiving Day, 1920. Berry Whitaker's Longhorns were decided underdogs to the Aggies who were within one game of their third straight unbeaten, untied, unscored-on season under Bible. On that occasion, as was the case 20 years later, Texas fashioned victory with a play that had been rehearsed only for a specific situation. A&M, leading 3-0, stopped the Longhorns at the goal on the final play of the third period. But minutes later it was fourth and seven at the Aggie 11.

The Texas backfield employed a shift from the box, and the ball was generally snapped on the first or second "hike." On this occasion Whitaker had told the Longhorns to shift on the second "hike," dropping the left end into the backfield and sending the right halfback onto the line of scrimmage.

Whitaker had hoped the move would cause the eager Aggies to jump offside. Though they did not fall for that, they lost track of tackle Tom Dennis, made eligible by the shift, and he went high into the air to pull down a pass from Bill Barry at the A&M three. Moments later Francisco Dominquez scored the winning touchdown for Texas' undefeated, untied season.

The 1968 club engineered big wins, including a last-minute, come-from-behind 26-20 win over Oklahoma and a trouncing of Tennessee in the Cotton Bowl to set the stage for the great 1969 team.

An earlier Cotton Bowl-bound Longhorn machine strengthened its national standing with a resounding upset in 1950. SMU, featuring Kyle Rote and Fred Benners, was the nation's No. 1 team when it rolled into Austin for a November confrontation with Texas, ranked seventh with a 14-13 loss to Oklahoma as its only blemish.

Texas partisans were so charged up that SMU coach Rusty Russell told Texas mentor Blair Cherry at a downtown press conference: "I sure hope your ball players aren't as fired up as these fans."

But in fact the team was fired up, holding SMU to minus 68 yards rushing to win 23-20. Byron Townsend scored twice, and Ben Tompkins completed 10 passes—one to Ben Proctor for a touchdown.

The excitement of the game, which attracted 67,000 fans with some 2,000 turned away at the gate, was tempered four days later when Cherry resigned.

A sparkling offensive display projected Texas back into the Cotton Bowl two years later for the second of three meetings with Tennessee. Though the Longhorns had two more games to play after the November 8, 1952, session with Baylor, the 35-33 win in Waco assured Texas of at least a share of the Southwest Conference crown.

Unlike the 1950 SMU game, the Longhorns were not in command all the way in this one. The all-SWC backfield of T. Jones, Gib Dawson, Billy Quinn, and Richard Ochoa did build a 21-13 half-time lead, and Ochoa burst 54 yards on the first play of the final quarter to put Texas out front 28-20. But Baylor went ahead 33-28 with five minutes left. The Longhorns were 74 yards from victory when Jones rallied his resourceful comrades into action. Quinn scored with 43 seconds left for the win.

Texas coach Ed Price said, "The team was poised enough, confident enough, and equipped with enough ability to meet the challenge. They were able to convert mistakes into success. You'll recall that critical play at midfield when Dawson fumbled a pitchout, picked it up on a bounce, and completed a pass to Quinn for a first down on the Baylor 47."

The 25-7 thumping Texas administered to SMU on November 1, 1930, ranks high on the big victory list. The Mustangs were fresh from a lopsided triumph over Indiana and a near miss against Notre Dame, while Texas had not conquered SMU in ten years.

The biggest achievement of the tremendous undefeated 1914 Longhorn team was a 32-7 conquest of Oklahoma in Dallas. Five members of that team were among the first 20 enshrined in the Longhorn Hall of Honor. They are Louis Jordan, Pete Edmond, K. L. Barry, Gus (Pig) Dittmar, and Clyde Littlefield.

Other great wins include the 1941 team's victory over

The University of Texas First Football Team

The undefeated 1893 club outscored its opponents 98-16 in compiling a 4-0 record. Front row from left to right: Dave Furman, Billy McLean, Manager Walter Crawford, Dick Lee, and Ad Day. Middle Row: Victor Moore, Paul McLane, and John Philip. Top Row: Ray McLane, captain James Morrison, Baby Myer, and Bill Ray. No recruiting pressure in those days.

A&M in College Station—the first in 18 years—and a 71-7 crushing of Oregon in 1941.

From The State Title To The Big Top

Picture the pampered modern athlete existing under the conditions of the very first University of Texas football captain—James Morrison.

Let us see now—there were no helmets in 1893. The stockings were heavy enough, but if you wanted shoes with cleats you had to nail them to the leather yourself. You wore long sleeve shirts and cotton-padded britches.

The games consisted of 90 minutes—no time out unless you wanted to drag a body off. The fringe benefits were a pat on the back...no apartments...no cars...no cash. You had to kind of like the game, flying wedge and all, to be playing it, don't you see.

The game plan was relatively simple—a straight ahead stampede. Texas went 4-0 that year, winning the so-called "state championship." Consider what Reginald D. Wentworth was paid in 1894 to take the club to a 6-1 record. Good ole Reggie got $325 that season. That would just about pay for the equipment of one modern football player in 1974. Or a guarantee to the 1895 team for playing Galveston—$250. That Texas team, by the way, scored 96 points to 0 for the other five teams on the schedule.

The pre-1900s at Texas were pretty much backwoodsy for the football team. But inflation struck even in those days. Before the 1900 season ticket prices were jacked from 50 cents to $1.00. What is it today? $6.00.

Huston Thompson took charge of the Longhorn football

The 1909 team, the only one that Dexter Draper—in the suit on the right—coached. They were 4-3-1.

club in 1900 and his team charged to a 6-0 season, whipping Oklahoma, Vanderbilt, Texas A&M, Missouri, Texas A&M, and the ever popular Kansas City Medics. This was the year that the student body voted in the orange and white colors.

Thompson was rather on the hard-nosed side, and there were no water breaks. Of course the modern idea now is water breaks along with a saline solution to keep away heat exhaustion. Anyone suffering a heat stroke in those days was considered out of shape.

The 1901 varsity which played five games in 13 days, beating Missouri, Oklahoma, and Texas A&M but falling to Kirksville and Kansas.

The tough Thompson was thought by some to be just this side of a mad man. How would you have liked to play five games in thirteen days? Well, Texas did it in 1901, winning three and losing two. Even Thompson was too tired to do much ranting after that 1,500 mile trip.

Thompson quit, and Texas went through a succession of not-so-hot seasons. John Hart was 6-3-1 in 1902 and gone... Ralph Hutchinson was 5-1-2 in 1903, 6-2 in 1904, and 5-4 in 1905...gone.

The Longhorns fielded a tremendous team under Henry Schenker in 1906, losing only to Vanderbilt to compile a 9-1 record.

Bleachers were built for the 1907 club under W. E. Metzenthin which went 6-1-1, a team almost two hours late for one game because of a train wreck that delayed departure from Austin.

The 1908 season was a bummer including a stunning 11-9 loss to little Southwestern, prompting Metzenthin to resign.

Dexter Draper assumed the reigns and he neither taught the forward pass or defense against it. Texas was 4-3-1, and Billy Wasmund got the call as mentor for the 1910 campaign but died before the 1911 season began.

Peppery Dave Allerdice started a career that lasted until 1915 and included one of the finest pre-modern era teams—the 1914 outfit which went 8-0. Led by Clyde Littlefield, Doc Neilson, and Hal Halbert, the team rolled up 358 points to but 21 for the opposition.

"That was a tremendous team," Littlefield recalled recently. "We had it all. We beat Mississippi 66-7. That will give you some idea what kind of a team it was."

Allerdice, concerned about the nit-picking of some Texas fans during the 6-3 season in 1915, resigned. It was a problem that has bugged some Longhorn coaches into the modern era, a few overzealous second-guessing fans.

Texas did not distinguish itself on the football field again until the 1918 season under Coach Bill Juneau. Of course it was during World War I, and the opponents were Penn Radio School and the Mabry Auto Mechanics—folks like that—but the 9-0 record looked good to Longhorn partisans.

The 1920 club under Berry Whitaker was a crack outfit

The undefeated Texas team of 1914.

with gritty Bully Gilstrap at halfback. A record crowd of 20,000 in Clark Field watched the 'Horns hook the Aggies 7-3 on Thanksgiving Day to seal a 9-0 record.

    The stiff arm of halfback Oscar Eckhardt spurred the Longhorns to an 8-0-1 slate under Doc Stewart in 1923 on a team that included such stars as Gilstrap and Abb Curtis. Eckhardt did not necessarily avoid tacklers. He attacked them much like a judo expert.

    Stewart never again fielded an undefeated team. After a brilliant beginning, he did not win often enough or big enough.

The undefeated Texas team of 1920.
That ushered in the Clyde Littlefield era of 1927.

The studio for picture snapping in 1909 was a wooden fence. Note background in this shot of fullback James T. Pearsons.

The 1913 outfit which was 7-1, losing only to Notre Dame and whipping Baylor 77-0. Coach Dave Allerdice who had a 33-7 record from 1911 to 1915 is on the back row, left.

Clyde Littlefield

It was 1912 when Clyde Littlefield tasted his first varsity game action for the University of Texas. Swift and rather large for that particular era—a gaudy 180 pounds—Littlefield became Texas' first consensus all-Southwest Conference player from his halfback position in 1915.

Littlefield played the game tough, and his hard-nosed attitude was to carry over into his coaching days at Texas. In seven years, from 1927 to 1933, his teams won two SWC titles and compiled a 44-18-6 ledger.

His theory was simple: "You had to be fair to the boys. Pat them on the back if it helps them. If they need a kick in the pants give it to them."

Players under Littlefield recall that if they made a mistake, Littlefield would be ready with his foot and say "Bend over." Such a practice in the modern era would stir letters to home and a Congressional investigation.

Littlefield said, "I see nothing wrong with hard work. Maybe that's what is wrong with the world today. The boys that need firing up don't get it."

Littlefield took over after Doc Stewart was sacked in an athletic department rift in 1927. Texas was to gain fame both in football and track under the salty Littlefield.

In his first season the Longhorns were 6-2-1 but held great promise for the future. One of the first things Littlefield did the next season was adopt the burnt orange jersies which Texas teams now use under Royal.

The great Clyde Littlefield. In seven years—from 1927 to 1933—his teams were 44-18-6. He was the first coach to use the five-man line as the standard defense in college football.

Ernie Koy, Sr., who was the star of the 1930-1932 Longhorn teams under Clyde Littlefield. Later, sons Ernie, Jr., and Ted were to shine in the backfield for Texas in the modern era under Coach Darrell Royal.

With some players wearing helmets and others disdaining them, the big game of the year was played before 45,000 fans against the Texas Aggies on Thanksgiving Day in Austin. Texas won 19-0 and the gate exceeded $80,000—a rather unheard of booty in those days for an athletic contest. The varsity had a

7-2 season.

In 1929 Texas was 5-2-1 and lost to the Aggies on Thanksgiving Day. But Littlefield sprang the five-man defensive front innovation on Southern Methodist the next year. SMU had defeated Texas in six consecutive tries before the strange defensive alignment confused Ray Morrison's offensive line on their blocking assignments.

Ernie Koy, Sr., and the rugged Harrison Stafford led the Longhorns to an 8-1-1 record and the SWC title in 1930. Littlefield raves to this day about the all-around play of Stafford. "He's the best all-around player I ever saw, and he could play for anybody and that includes all the teams of today," Littlefield said.

Stafford recalled: "You were absolutely scared not to give your best under Coach Littlefield. He knew instantly if a player was dogging it. You went all out at all times."

The 1931 season was a 6-4 disappointment, but the first of the tremendous Texas breakaway backs made his appearance in 1932—Bohn Hilliard, whose feats included a 95-yard punt return against Oklahoma.

The year of 1932 was an 8-2 season, but Littlefield said: "We wanted to win the Rice game most of all because they had beaten us two years and we had received some criticism." Texas took out the Owls 18-6. The only losses that year were 13-6 to Centenary and 14-0 to TCU.

Texas was 4-5-2 in a miserable 1933 season, and Littlefield resigned but stayed on as track coach. He coached track for 41 seasons, and his teams won 25 SWC titles.

The 1926 team. Note the use of some semblance of shoulder padding.

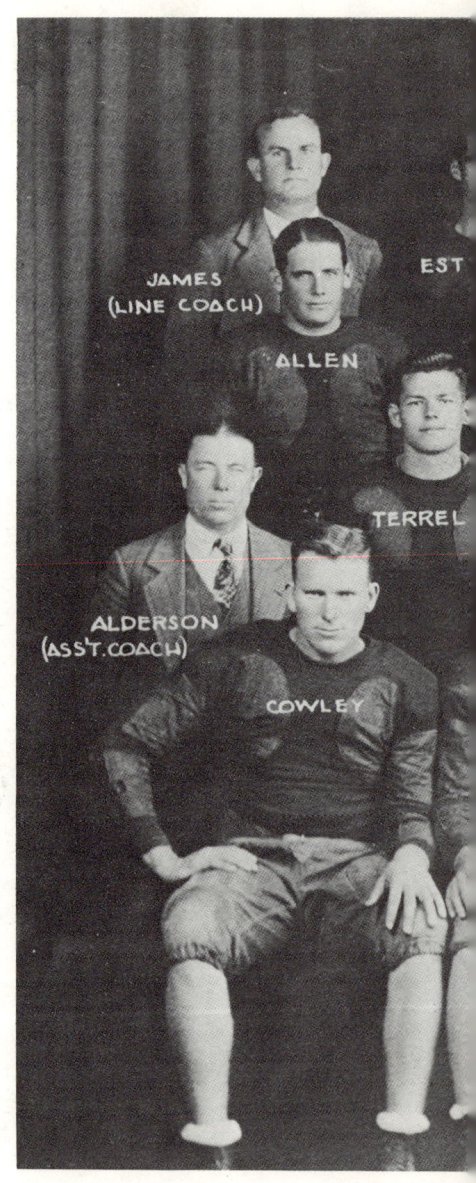

1934-1936 And A Stroke Of Glory

Jack Chevigny, a muscular Indianan who scored a key touchdown in a Notre Dame upset of Army as the Irish "Won one for the Gipper," got the last shot at taking Texas to greatness before the D. X. Bible era. Chevigny, ironically, gave Texas football one of its finest hours by stunning his alma mater, Notre Dame, in South Bend.

A tough taskmaster in the Bible mold, Chevigny took over from Littlefield in 1934. With a contract signed for the princely sum of $4,200, Chevigny converted the Texas offense into the Notre Dame box shift out of the T-formation.

The Longhorns struggled in their opener to defeat Texas Tech 12-6, and always-awesome Notre Dame loomed on the schedule next October 6, 1934. Bohn Hilliard fled 94 yards for a touchdown against the Red Raiders, and it was to be something of an omen for the ambush of the Irish.

Not since 1896 had the Irish suffered an opening game defeat. They were not exactly sweating this one, either, offering the Longhorns a mere $5,000 guarantee if they would like to show up.

J. Neils Thompson, now the University of Texas faculty representative for athletics, was a reserve on that 1934 team, but he recalls the Chevigny pregame speech. Chevigny spoke of the late Notre Dame coach Knute Rockne and of his dying father and of his mother, who was buried not far from South Bend.

"You can't imagine how fired up we were after we heard

Texas recruits 'em young.

the speech," recalls Thompson.

But the wily Chevigny was not to rely on oratory alone. He had an opening seven he was going to roll at the "Luck of the Irish."

Notre Dame had lost its regular right halfback who died in the summer of 1934. Chevigny reasoned that the inexperienced replacement might be a tad nervous.

Texas practiced kickoffs to the deep back on the theory that tenseness might turn his fingers to buttered noodles. Notre Dame's George Melinkovich, the star Irish back, switched positions with the newcomer at the last second and fumbled in his haste. Jack Gray, who was to become an all-American in basketball and a highly successful coach, captured the fumble at the Notre Dame 18.

The Chevigny gambit had not worked exactly as planned, but it at least created confusion among the usually poised Irish.

The gutty 170-pound Hilliard followed guard Joe Smartt

eight yards for the touchdown on the fourth play after the numbed Irish lost the ball. Hilliard kicked the extra point, and Texas held on before the crowd of 33,000 to prevail 7-6. On that same day Rice upset Purdue and Southwest football had arrived and so had Chevigny.

Texas finished with a 7-2-1 record, losing to always salty Centenary and Rice.

The Longhorns sagged sadly in 1935 with a 4-6 ledger, closing with three consecutive losses to TCU, Arkansas, and Texas A&M. Supporters began to wonder where the Chevigny magic had gone.

Chevigny drew criticism for recruiting out of state, and his pregame speeches began to strike some players as a bit on the corny side. Although Texas beat Oklahoma in 1936, the Longhorns were humiliated by Minnesota 47-19.

A hero in 1934, Chevigny was through and tendered his "resignation." He died in World War II as a lieutenant on Iwo Jima.

Chevigny brought Texas a taste of the big time. The coach to follow him, Dana X. Bible, was to etch that tradition in cement.

Texas hit the big-time jackpot on this 1934 touchdown by Bohn Hilliard against Notre Dame in South Bend, Indiana. Texas won the game 7-6 as the football giants of the Midwest and East became aware of a budding power in the Southwest.

How It Was

When J. Neils Thompson reminisces about University of Texas football, it is tinged with something bordering on science fiction. A child in the depression, the 1974 chairman of the UT athletic council finds himself staring at million dollar budgets as the costs of maintaining sports skyrockets.

"There were virtually no scholarships when I played," says Thompson, the reserve end behind the great Jack Gray in the early 1930s. "Sometimes they could get a job for you, but there weren't many jobs in the bottom of the depression. If you were lucky to get a job, it was usually janitorial work. It's a far cry from that now."

After long, hard practices Thompson remembers dinners in a jammed dining hall where "you had to pay your own way. You really had to love the game. I know—I was taking engineering. It was extremely hard to play football and keep up with my studies."

Thompson played under Clyde Littlefield and Jack Chevigny, and just about the time he was making an impression on Littlefield along came Ernie Koy.

"I'll never forget that collision," Thompson says. "I tried to tackle Ernie head-on in a scrimmage, and his knee caught me flush on the jaw. I was knocked out five or ten minutes."

Thompson has not liked soup much since.

"The doctor wired my broken jaw, and I had to take soup through a straw for weeks," he recalls. "I was lost that season."

Under Chevigny, Thompson played little because of Gray

and the fact that Thompson told the coach he was going to forego the final year of eligibility to graduate on time.

This was the era of the rah-rah locker room oratory, and Thompson says Chevigny's speech before the 1934 Notre Dame will remain a classic.

Thompson says that "Chevigny, of course, played his collegiate ball at Notre Dame and claimed that Knute Rockne wanted him to be the next coach of the Irish. Rockne was killed in a plane crash, but Chevigny never got the call.

"Chevigny said that he was the heir to the throne...that a great man's wish didn't come true...and that we could make up for it by defeating Notre Dame that day—you know sort of show 'em what they missed.

"I never heard anything like it. But the speech had its impact, and we went all out. Chevigny kept trying the same thing throughout the season, and it later wore thin."

That 7-6 victory over Notre Dame is noted as one of the historical prestige moments for Southwest football.

Speaking of today's athletics Thompson says that, "We must entertain because it's the entertainment dollar that sustains us...It's all show business now. Our style of living has changed, and so has football and the youngsters who play it."

Thompson is not all that fired up to go back to "the good ole days." Not when he sees a modern face mask that would have probably saved him a broken jaw.

The Leather Helmet Era

The pre-Bible and Royal eras at the University of Texas hold special memories for thousands of Longhorn alumni.

"We had just as much spirit or maybe more back then," proclaims Clayton Hickerson, the night editor of the *Associated Press* in Dallas who was the class of 1931 secretary-treasurer. "I remember we tore an old World War I barracks down so we would have enough wood for a bonfire before the A&M game."

Texas football began on Thanksgiving Day, 1893, when the Austinites conquered Dallas 18-16 at the Fair Grounds behind Captain James Morrison. Since that fine start, Texas has lost just eight games in eighty openers.

R. D. Wentworth stepped in as coach in 1895, and Texas was to have a different mentor each season until 1900-1901 when S. H. Thompson lasted for two years. Texas did an amazing thing under Thompson. The Longhorns played five games in thirteen days. Between November 16 and November 28 the 1901 team beat Missouri 11-0, lost to Kirksville 48-0 (Yep, Kirksville), lost to Kansas 12-0, whipped Oklahoma 11-0, and tromped Texas A&M 32-0.

In 1903 Texas got the nickname "Longhorns" from Alex Weisburg, editor-in-chief of the student newspaper *The Texan*.

The Longhorns won their first Southwest Conference title—first of nineteen—under Berry Whitaker. In 1920 Clyde Littlefield brought the Longhorns two SWC titles in the seven years he coached from 1927 to 1933.

Although the late Jack Chevigny did not win a

Coach Bible enjoying a chat with some of the players wearing the finest in football finery in the 1940s.

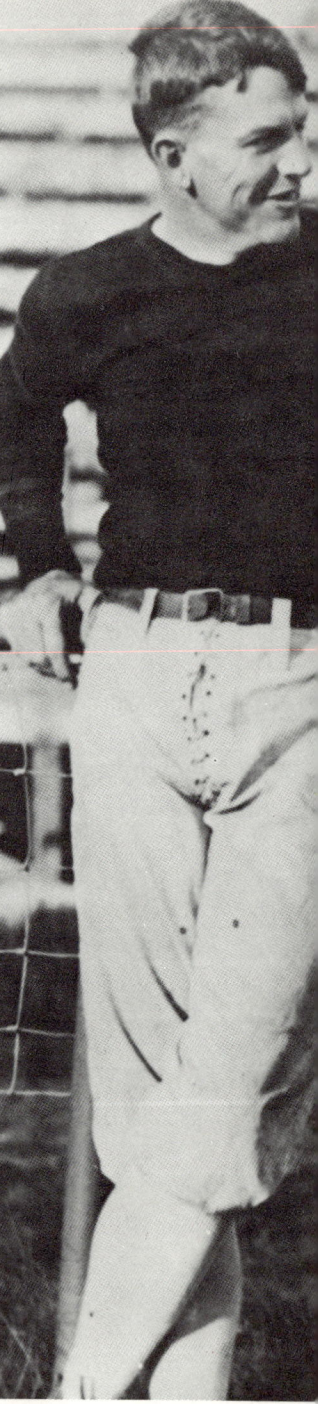

championship before Bible took over in 1937, he projected SWC football into national prominence with a 7-6 upset of Notre Dame in South Bend, Indiana. Notre Dame had never lost a season opener until that game.

Chevigny, who was to be killed on Iwo Jima in World War II, directed his team to boot the opening kickoff into the hands of an inexperienced Notre Dame back who promptly fumbled at the Irish 18, and Jack Gray, a starting end for the 'Horns, pounced on the ball. Bohn Hilliard scored the touchdown four plays later and added what proved to be the winning point.

While the 1914 Longhorn team was the highest scoring Texas team of them all with the likes of Littlefield, Gus (Pig) Dittmar, Louis Jordan, Pete Edmond, K. L. Berry—all enshrined in the Longhorn Hall of Honor—the 1920 club will always stand out.

It was the first Texas team to go unbeaten through conference warfare.

An unheard of crowd of 20,000 poured into old Clark Field Thanksgiving Day to watch Texas come from behind to nip the Texas Aggies 7-3 on a fourth quarter touchdown by Francisco Dominquez.

Whitaker said that he did not realize the significance of the victory until later.

"You see, it was my first year as a head coach, and I had not experienced defeat. I did not think too much of it at the time," Whitaker said.

In 1930 Texas downed Southern Methodist 25-7 in a game that saw Littlefield use a five-man line as a standard defense for the first time in the history of collegiate football. Ox Emerson, Ox Blanton, Dutch Bumgarten, and Lester Peterson were the bulwarks of the line while the 'Horns fielded a tremendous backfield of Dexter Shelley, Bull Elkins, Ernie Koy, and Harrison Stafford. Koy, of course, besides being an all-time great himself, sired two sons, Ernie Jr. and Ted, who were later to star at Texas.

Stafford was perhaps the most vicious blocker from his wingback position that a Texas team has ever known.

"Harrison made the most devastating block on Johnny Vaught I ever saw made in college football," Littlefield recalls. "Johnny was playing for TCU and was coming down under a punt. He apparently didn't see Harrison, but you could hear the sound all over the stadium. To this day when I see Johnny (former head football coach at Mississippi) he just shakes his head and says 'Now, Coach, I know what you're going to say—do I remember...'"

Stafford recently reminisced how tough it was to work, be a student, and play football in those days. Stafford, now a rancher in Edna, Texas, says, "I tried to quit once, and my brother kicked my tail all the way back to Austin. I remember the first job they gave me to help pay my tuition—cleaning out spittoons in Gregory Gymnasium. There were a lot of spittoons. I got off that duty as soon as I could, I'll tell you."

He says in a way it saddens him to see the departure of one platoon football.

"Don't get me wrong, I love to see the wide open offenses of today, and I'm glad that a lot of kids are getting to play," Stafford says. "But it's so costly, and I'd hate to see college football price itself right out of the game. I love the game dearly, but I don't see why a real athlete can't play offense and defense, too."

Stafford can be forgiven his nostalgia trips just like any Texas fan who wants to argue that the Jack Crain of the late 1930s was every bit as good a broken field runner as James Saxton of the 1960s; that Stafford could give Roosevelt Leaks blocking lessons; that James Street was a better clutch performer than Bobby Layne, etc.

It makes each autumn something special on the Forty Acres. It has since 1893.

Dana Xeonophon Bible

D. X. Bible is waiting in his driveway at the end of a winding country road on the outskirts of Austin this unusually bright and balmy February day. It is his eighty-second year, yet there is a firm handshake for his visitor who wants to relive the days of Longhorn football when they went from the laugh of the league to the bully boys.

There is a tour of the Bible home while wife Dorothy prepares coffee and, although he is unable to play himself, Bible cannot resist a tee-to-green look at the treacherous Par 3 stretching the width of his backyard. He is saying something about the out-of-bounds on the left and the grandkids, but it is all somehow lost in the presence of the man.

They say his parents gave him his middle name after a famous Greek general when Bible was born in Jefferson City, Tennessee, in 1891. The thought occurs that the Greek general probably never won half the battles D. X. Bible did.

Bible simply saved football at the University of Texas in its darkest hours—not once but twice. His record is chiseled in the National Football Hall of Fame—fourteen conference champions in thirty-four seasons of coaching in such institutions as Nebraska, Texas A&M, and finally Texas, where he was 63-31-3 in ten years with three SWC titles.

It is interesting to note that the Carson-Newman College graduate played for the first team he coached—Brandon Prep School. Later he was to coach at Mississippi College from 1913-1915 where he had three winning seasons, at LSU in 1916 where he was 5-1, at A&M from 1917 to 1928, and at Nebraska from 1929 to 1936 before heeding the call to Texas.

"Bless your heart you have to be lucky to get a job as the head coach of a college because you know hundreds of coaches still in high school who are qualified...it's timing and luck," he says.

You sit down at the kitchen table with him and his wife and say, "But Coach Bible, it's not luck when you have only two losing seasons in thirty-four years, is it?"

Bible smiles. Here is the same man that the famed Knute Rockne recommended at Nebraska. And here was the same man who later had the good judgment to recommend Darrell Royal for the Longhorn job.

Texas came after Bible hard in 1937. The school had not captured a championship since 1930 during the Clyde Littlefield reign. Jack Chevigny had been the coach for the last three, fruitless years.

"I don't know who got the most publicity at the time...me or the Duke and Duchess of Windsor at the time he was abdicating," Bible says. "They wouldn't take 'no' for an answer. I told them if I came I needed several things. I wanted the most outstanding high school coach in Texas. That was Blair Cherry...I wanted the outstanding junior college coach—that was Bully Gilstrap. Those were my assistants and great ones."

Bible continues, "Jack Gray and Ed Price handled the freshmen, and Littlefield handled the junior varsity and recruiting. We went after Texas boys. We figured they would have more pride playing for a school in their own state."

The start of the "Bible Plan" was not an impressive one. Texas was 1-5 in both 1937 and 1938.

"I asked for five years, and it didn't take quite that long to get things turned around," Bible remembers.

He says a long touchdown run by Jack Crain in 1939 was the start of an uplift in Longhorn football fortunes.

"Arkansas was leading 13-7 in the final minute of play, and fullback R. P. Patrick hit Crain with a short pass and he raced sixty-seven yards for the touchdown with sixteen seconds to play," Bible says. "Then Jack kicked the extra point for victory."

Writers have hailed that victory the renaissance of football

Named after a Greek general, the legendary D. X. Bible.

at Texas.

"It was the year without question that we started moving," Bible says. "Crain was a wonderful, explosive back. The Crain and Pete Layden group...they were something special."

In 1940 Texas upset conference champion Texas A&M with some Bible trickery.

"It was such an important game because A&M was headed to the Rose Bowl if they won," Bible says. "We had a play planned after the opening kickoff if we got the ball, and it worked beautifully. Layden was put in at tailback, and Crain, ordinarily the tailback, went to fullback. Crain slipped to the sideline, and Layden threw the ball diagonally across the field. It went for a long gain, and we eventually scored."

In 1941 the first great team under Bible had a chance to go to the Rose Bowl. Texas had a game left with Oregon after beating Texas A&M. The Rose Bowl offered Texas the trip if the Longhorns would cancel the Oregon game. Oregon State, the West Coast representative, had defeated the Ducks 20-16, and the bowl officials did not want to take the chance Texas might lose to Oregon after getting the invite. Bible said no thanks, and Texas promptly crushed Oregon 71-7.

"In a way I guess you can say we would have had a pretty good chance against Oregon State," Bible says.

Texas won the 1943 Cotton Bowl 14-7 over Georgia Tech, tied Randolph Field 7-7 in 1945, and defeated Missouri 40-27 in the 1945 Cotton Bowl under Bible.

Bible organized a state-wide association in fifteen Texas districts during his tenure to encourage prospects to come to the school. He standardized campus employment so that athletes could earn their school expenses within conference rules and still play football.

In 1947 Bible stepped into the athletic director's role, and Cherry took over. In 1951 Cherry resigned although he had a fine 32-10-1 record. Price coached six years, but a 1-9 record in 1956 signaled another spiral in Texas' football fortunes.

"Blair and Ed were fine coaches, but they didn't beat Oklahoma enough and that always causes concern among the alumni," Bible says. "It's an important game, and there is a lot of emphasis on it."

The 1939 team that changed the football philosophy at Texas from defeat to victory. The little general, D. X. Bible, is in the sweat suit at the far left.

Coach D. X. Bible on the first team he coached, Brandon Prep. He is the one with the football in the middle.

It was time for the five-foot-eight "Little General" to act again.

Bobby Dodd of Georgia Tech was the prime candidate for both the athletic directorship and the head coaching job, but he turned it down. It was decided that a young, up-and-coming coach was needed, with Bible staying on for five years in an advisory capacity with Ed Ollie as the athletic director.

Dodd suggested a call to a young coach at Washington who had only a 5-5 record the 1956 season but was an excellent teacher and recruiter. The results of that telephone call from Bible to Royal can be found on other pages of this book.

"Darrell has served this institution so well," Bible says. "So much depends on recruiting, and Darrell is the best. He keeps his program clean...and tells it like it is. If you don't have

Dana X. Bible—a study in concentration even on the practice field.

a good policy and things aren't going well, then some of your people (alumni) get offsides. This can hurt you."

Bible is looking out the window now as Dorothy goes for the mail and reminisces about the difference in coaching today and decades ago.

"There are so many coaches now, and so much money is spent," Bible says. "Bless your life, it's hard to keep up with the finances. So many schools are in financial trouble.

"A head coach used to be part of everything done on the field. That's impossible now with the two platoon system. Take that Mike Campbell on defense. Why he's like a head coach. It's getting where a head coach is like the President of the United States. People just tell him about what's in the newspaper because he doesn't have time to read it. But the responsibility is the same. If something goes wrong, it's Darrell Royal not Mike Campbell."

Bible says that it is a fine thing that so many boys get to play football.

"We only used thirteen or fourteen when we beat A&M in 1940," Bible says. "My son lettered in football, but back when I was coaching he probably wouldn't have done it. He did a strong job on defense, but he wasn't fast enough to play both ways."

Bible continues, "The game has opened up. There's more deception and ball control. But there's one thing we did that was really good back in my day...we had a good kicking game. We could kick for those corners, and we'd kick a lot on early downs. You never liked to own the ball in your end of the field."

There is time for a visit to the Bible trophy room now, and the trophies and plaques are staggering—President of the American Football Coaches Association, member of National Football Rules Committee twenty-seven years, charter member of the Football Coaches Association, member of the Helms Hall of Fame and National Hall of Fame, winner of the Amos Alonzo Stagg Award, Who's Who in America, Longhorn Hall of Honor, etc.

The gentle, baldheaded man points to a piece of philosophy by a long-lost poet named Marden. It reads: "Give me a man who holds on when others let go, who pushes ahead when

Pete Layden going up and over for the only touchdown in a 7-0 victory over the Texas Aggies in 1940. Layden was the leading rusher in an 8-2 season, the best for the 'Horns since 1932.

Roy Dale McKay—considered by D. X. Bible as the finest punter in Texas history.

others turn back; who stiffens up when others retreat; who knows no such word as 'can't' or 'give up'; and I will show you a man who will win in the end."

"That," he says, "is the way I've felt about athletics and life."

In the semi-jaded society of today, that might be ripped-off as a bit corny. It worked wonders for a little man who never won a national football championship but kept the foundation built for the day when the University of Texas became the proudest power in the land.

"I guess I've been influenced by a lot of people, but I'd like to finish and be as well thought of as Mr. Bible," says Darrell Royal.

Last entrance of 1941 Seniors Compliments of the Longhorn Band.

The All-American Water Boy And Friend Bobby

In the University of Texas Football Hall of Honor, "Rooster" Andrews is the smallest Longhorn. But in the proud tradition of "Hook 'Em Horns", orange-lit towers, and mascot Bevo, the four-foot-eleven and three-fourth 120-pound Andrews stands as a symbol of turning a limitation into an asset.

Billy M. Andrews was one of the most colorful characters in the history of Texas football from the night he fell out of a tree catching a fighting cock to dropkicks which stunned the opposition. He served as manager of Longhorn athletic teams for four years starting in 1941, managed the college all-Stars at the annual Chicago grid classic for five years, and performed one year for the West in the East-West game. His roommates at Texas included Malcolm Kutner, Joe Parker, Roy Dale McKay, and Bobby Layne—all destined for stardom.

Layne, the golden arm of Texas gridiron annals, admired Andrews for his fiesty manner, and they became fast friends.

"You forget about his smallness pretty quick," Layne said. "Before long he becomes as big as you."

Andrews, who was a manager at Dallas Woodrow Wilson High School, was offered a scholarship at Texas A&M, but Kutner, an all-American end on Texas' 1941 "wonder team," persuaded Coach D. X. Bible to interview Andrews.

"I was impressed with his enthusiasm, and he was later to become the best manager I ever saw," Bible recalled.

Andrews, who owns a sporting goods store in Austin, got

Rooster Andrews, the all-American "Water Boy" and his drop-kicking style. Note most of the spectators are larger.

the tag "Rooster" one dark night in a tree near Clark Field. Jack Crain, McKay, "Bo" Cohenour, and "Buddy" Jungmichael snatched freshman Andrews out of bed and ordered him up the tree to get the rooster, "Walter." What Andrews did not know was that "Walter" was a fierce fighting cock.

"I was scared of height anyway and could use only one arm to climb because the other held a flashlight," Andrews said. "That son-of-a-gun just ate me up. I fell out of the tree with "Walter" and smashed my arm. Those seniors took "Walter" to Elgin and made $300.00 that night."

Andrews' dropkicks caught the eye of Bible in practice, and Andrews won a "kickoff" contest before the 1943 game with Texas Christian.

"Coach Bible always held a contest during the week, and the winner got to kick in the game," Andrews said. "I won and was just a little shocked."

Texas whipped TCU 42-6 with Rooster kicking two extra points.

"It made (TCU) Coach Dutch Meyer madder than hell," Rooster said. "He rushed out on the field and asked me, 'What are you doing here?' The TCU coaches thought we were making fun of their team. Flem Hall of the *Fort Worth Star-Telegram* really roasted Bible. I remember he said if I was the extra point kicker, let's see Bible put me in against Texas A&M.

"I kicked an extra point that put us ahead 14-13 of A&M and we went on to win the game. I got a nice letter later from Coach Meyer, and Mr. Hall conceded that I deserved to play.

"I used to run out on the field with the water bucket and my helmet on," Andrews says. "You never knew when we were going to score those days with Bobby in there, and I wanted to be ready."

Andrews and his "roomie" Layne were the talk of the Southwest Conference. National writers interviewed Andrews and dubbed him the "all-American Water Boy."

Occasionally Andrews and Layne would pull off a fake kick with Andrews passing to Layne in the left end zone. It worked time and again until the year SMU all-American Doak Walker, who went to Highland Park High School with Layne, came along. Walker often visited Layne and Andrews in Austin, and around a beer or two they would tell the Doaker of ambushing the opposition with this trick play. The next year Walker went to SMU.

"We hadn't used the trick play all year until we met SMU and decided the time was ripe," Andrews said. "We huddled up, and I sneaked a peek to make sure Doak wasn't lined up on the side. I wanted to throw the ball to Bobby. Everything looked good. The snap was perfect, and I faked the kick and cocked my arm to pass to Bobby. There was Doak standing in the end zone with a smile on his face, just waving. I had to ground the dang thing."

Andrews was not much of a field goal kicker—his longest was eighteen yards—but he was invaluable to Bible as a team holler guy and also keeping tabs on Layne.

"We really didn't get away with much around Coach Bible," Andrews said. "We were darned scared of him...in fact, right now I wouldn't want him to see me smoking."

Andrews said, "Oh, we got thrown in jail once for popping some giant firecrackers on the Fourth of July. We flooded a dorm out once and had to write a four-page single space apology letter."

Andrews said Layne was almost unbelieveably calm before a game.

"It was just like he was in a beer joint playing shuffle board or something," Andrews says. "Come kickoff, he'd just go out and whip your tail."

Rooster recalls Layne was hell on offensive linemen. "I remember one game when a guy ran by Harlan Wetz of New Braunfels and really blasted Bobby. Bobby really chewed him out. He said, 'Wetz, you big, fat, sloppy SOB, you shouldn't be playing football...you should be back in New Braunfels eating your momma's sausage and drinking her room temperature beer.'

"Wetz knocked the guy down every time after that he was so mad."

Rooster and Layne were always in some sort of minor mischief.

"It almost cost us the baseball championship one year," Rooster says. "I pushed Bobby, and he cut his foot. It took six stitches, and we were supposed to play A&M the next day for the title. We didn't dare let Coach Bibb Faulk know about it.

We wrapped it up, and I fed Bobby a six-pack of beer during the game behind the dugout. We won, and the coach never knew about it. Bobby was an incredible pitcher. He never lost a conference game."

Andrews' greatest athletic thrill came on the baseball field when he delivered a game-winning hit against Texas A&M after he had been sent to the plate to get a walk.

"Ed Price was the coach," Andrews said. "He didn't say a word—just shook my hand."

The late C. O. "Ox" Higgins, an all-America tackle at Texas in 1927, offered Rooster a job with C&S Sporting Goods Company, and in 1946 Andrews began to sell athletic equipment. He now owns the store.

One of Andrews' few disappointments at Texas was that he could not enter the war because of his size.

"I kept trying to stretch my frame out on a shower rod, but it just wouldn't work," Andrews says. "I never could get that last one-fourth of an inch."

To this day Rooster and the Blond Bomber still hoist a glass in honor of the good ole days.

"Not many people really ever got to know the real Bobby," Andrews said. "Basically he's a shy person. For three years we were inseparable. He would have a date with Carol (now his wife), and I would go, too. I spent a lot of nights just walking in the woods while they sparked."

Because of his size Rooster Andrews could not spend much time being shy.

It's like a friend says of the only "all-American Water Boy" in collegiate football history: "God only made him five-feet tall, but it was all buzzsaw!"

The Mission Kid

To this day Tom Landry still remembers the astonishment in Bobby Layne's eyes some twenty-seven years ago. Landry, the only coach the Dallas Cowboys of the National Football League have known, was a fullback and the incomparable Layne was quarterback. Southern Methodist led 14-13 deep in the fourth quarter. It was fourth and one on the SMU 35. Layne barked Landry's number and broke the huddle. The crowd surged to its feet, Layne took the center snap, wheeled...and... where the heck was Landry?

"I slipped on the play and fell flat on my pants," Landry recalls. "I can still remember the expression on Bobby's face. He just stood there holding the ball, and I couldn't get up...it was such a helpless feeling...there went the drive...there went the ballgame...I'll never forget it."

Landry and Layne can laugh about the incident now, but it was the only game the 1947 Longhorns lost and they later put a 27-7 knot on Alabama in the Sugar Bowl.

"My greatest experience came the next year," Landry says. "I started the year by having some compacted wisdom teeth yanked, and it took me to the Texas Christian game before I regained my strength because of the poison in my system. We went to Miami to play Georgia in the Orange Bowl, and everybody said we had a second-rate team. We beat 'em good, and I had my best game—gained over 100 yards."

Landry was a D. X. Bible recruit from Mission High School in the Lower Rio Grande Valley which long carried more of a

Tom Landry displays his running style when he was a 190-pound fullback.

Malcolm Kutner gained the first all-America recognition from his end post for Texas in 1941. Teammate Chal Danniel also was named to the national dream team that year.

reputation for its citrus groves than football players.

"Back in those days you had to have a Texas-ex recommend you, and Doc Newhouse of Mission was an alumnus," Landry said. "He got me into Texas. Our area wasn't as respected as most in the state, but Jackie Fields, who was from Mission, was playing for Coach Bible and that helped. Austin was the closest of the Southwest Conference schools, and it was plenty big enough for me. I hadn't been any place to speak of."

Landry was highly impressed by Bible.

"He was a great orator and motivator," Landry says. "Some of his locker-room talks were pure Knute Rockne. But after the war everybody dropped that and tried to become mechanically efficient."

Landry says that Bible was "A great organizer and the greatest recruiter I ever saw."

In his junior year Blair Cherry took over the Texas team, and Landry found himself as a No. 2 quarterback behind Layne and a reserve in the secondary.

"I broke a thumb against Oklahoma, and since it was my right thumb the quarterback king days were over...they moved me to fullback," says Landry who played at a not-so-awesome 190 pounds.

Landry eventually worked his way into the starting lineup and gained 100 yards against North Carolina. The job was permanently his.

Landry says he has never really tried to emulate either of his college coaches in the professional ranks.

"You are what you are," says Landry. "I just know I'm glad I went to Texas...it's been good to me."

Tom Landry went on to star for the New York Giants and innovate the 4-3 defense in professional football.

He is the most successful coach the University of Texas ever graduated. And he can understand when one of his fullbacks has a pratfall.

The Blond Bomber

Almost three decades after he had terrorized the Southwest Conference with his pinpoint bombing, Bobby Layne, Texas' deadliest gunner, drew the most backslaps, handshakes, and even Bob Hope's needle at a recent Texas Sports Hall of Fame reunion. Layne with his swashbuckling flair on the field and his curfew-stretching off of it is a legitimate, American gridiron folklore, Grade-A hero. They remember Layne for his guts and mostly for being a winner.

"Some of the players today forget what they are on the field for...and that's TO WIN," Layne says. "Heck, the money never made that big a difference to me in pro ball. But I just couldn't stand to lose."

Although he had a reputation as a hell-raiser, Layne was a winner—at Dallas Highland Park High School, at Texas, and in professional football—all fifteen years of play for pay.

And he always gave credit to his teammates, saying, "You're nuthin' without those ten big brothers."

But back to the Sports Hall of Fame awards dinner. Hope is on the podium now, and of all the Texas sports stars in attendance which included Ben Hogan, Byron Nelson, Doak Walker, Kyle Rote, etc., he picks on Layne...

"It is thrilling to look at these athletes and see what training, discipline, and hard work will do...and then to see Bobby Layne."

Laughter.

"Layne, you know, was the innovator of the x-rated

huddle." Hope giggles. "He's the only football player who had a water bucket on the sideline with a head on it."

Layne's idea of professional football was to relax between workouts and games with beers and teammates.

"If you're going to play twenty games, you sure as heck better have some fun in the meantime," he recalled.

With Layne as the chairman in Detroit, the team would discuss its troubles between rounds of chug-a-lug games. There was a close knit group that gathered each Monday in the same pub.

"We settled all our troubles together instead of scattering out at different bars," Layne says.

While Layne laughed at Hope's jokes, there were times when he felt he was under a giant microscope...which is why he lives a quiet, private life with his beautiful wife, Carol, in Lubbock, Texas.

He once told Gary Cartwright, who worked at the time for the *Dallas Morning News*: "Most of the stuff written about me was an exaggeration or a darn lie. I could go into a place and have a few beers, and people who had been in there drinking ten or twelve martinis would say I was staggering drunk just because I was Bobby Layne. If I didn't have a family, I wouldn't of cared. But what were they going to think? Didn't anyone imagine they had feelings? All the press gave a darn about was selling papers."

Layne concluded, "You can ask any teammate or coach I ever had about it...I was always ready for a game physically and mentally."

Rooster Andrews, who was Layne's roomie in college, says simply, "Bobby is probably the most misunderstood person in sports history. He's basically a shy person."

Layne has mellowed and chatted freely with sportswriters and broadcasters at the Hall of Fame gathering. He had a warning for both college and pro football: "Nothing has changed in football except they are overexposing the game now. You can't have Canadian football on Wednesday, a kid playing ball on Friday, colleges on Saturday, and the pros on Sunday and Monday. You know how many days of the week that is? Wives rule the world, you know, and they're getting tired of it."

Robert Lawrence Layne has been the measuring stick for

every quarterback in the Southwest Conference since he graduated in the late 1940s. He played under two coaches, D. X. Bible and Blair Cherry, and was equally effective under the different systems. Layne was a tailback and a fullback in the Bible style of play and a T-formation quarterback under Cherry.

"Bobby Layne simply was the most gifted ball handler and passer I've ever seen," said Bible. "He was a fantastic competitor yet always had his head in the game. I never saw him lose his poise."

The six-foot-one, 196-pound Layne's passing bordered on magic, but he was gifted in almost every phase of the game.

"He was a tremendous quick-kicker, a good runner, and an able defensive man," Bible says. "In 1945 he led the conference in passing, scoring, and punting."

In the 1946 Cotton Bowl game against Missouri, Bible saw Layne complete eleven of twelve passes. The incomplete pass should have been caught, and Layne figured in the scoring of all six Texas touchdowns in a 40-27 victory.

Layne was awesome from the day he stepped off the campus at Highland Park High School in Dallas.

"He was a natural...just a natural," Bible says.

In 1947 Layne blossomed under Cherry's T-formation. He paced the SWC in passing and overshadowed Alabama's great Harry Gilmer in the 1948 Sugar Bowl as the Longhorns downed the Crimson Tide 27-7.

There had been skepticism that Layne could not switch from the single wing to the T. After he had proved he could do so successfully, the Orange bloods worried about rainy days.

The 1947 Arkansas-Texas game put those fears to the woodshed. The field was a quagmire, yet Texas won 21-6 and Layne threw only five short passes.

"Layne doesn't need to pass," one Arkansas player said later. "His quarterbacking alone beat us."

Layne completed college with a .535 passing percentage and averaged 15.2 yards per completed pass. In baseball he posted a 39-7 record and was 28-0 for his career against conference opponents.

After disdaining a professional baseball career, Layne played for the Chicago Bears and the New York Bulldogs. The

The great 1947 team which beat Alabama in the Sugar Bowl. Bobby Layne is No. 22, and Tom Landry is No. 24.

glory years were at Detroit where he quarterbacked the Lions to National Football League titles in 1952 and 1953. When he finished his career at Pittsburgh, he had completed passes for more than FIFTEEN MILES.

Perhaps Layne was best summed up by a golf professional, of all people.

"Bobby plays any game...golf, gin rummy, name it...like it was the world championship," says Gene Mitchell.

Carol Layne, who married Bobby in his junior year at Texas, says, "He has to win...even when our boys were little he had to beat them at checkers."

Company Men

They were good company men, Blair Cherry and Ed Price, and served their boss, D. X. Bible, and the University of Texas well. In ten years between 1947 until 1956 they combined for three Southwest Conference titles. However, hitting .300 is not good enough at Texas.

Cherry came up from the assistant ranks, as did Price. The grey-thatched Cherry perhaps had the misfortune of filling the shoes of the legendary Bible. In only four years beginning with the 1947 campaign, Cherry managed an excellent 32-10-1 record with one conference title. His Southwest Conference ledger showed an 18-5-1 mark. So why did Cherry quit?

Three losses to Oklahoma could serve as openers. The alumni did not like that. Cherry got telephone calls at 3:00 a.m. wondering why he did not pass more or why the Longhorns passed so much. Cherry did not like that.

So, in the middle of the 1950 season, as his team steamrolled to a SWC title and a No. 3 ranking nationally, Cherry told his post-midnight quarterbacking "friends" that as far as he was concerned they could run the team.

It was ironic that one-point losses by his 1947 team to Southern Methodist and to Oklahoma in 1950 cost him national championships and silencing of the wolves. The 1947 team crunched Alabama soundly in the Sugar Bowl.

The 1948 team lost its last three games but shocked Georgia in the Orange Bowl. The 1949 team dipped to 6-4, and a 14-13 loss to Oklahoma started the grumbling.

Good Luck From the Doaker
Doak Walker (left), former all-America back from Southern Methodist University and now playing with the professional Detroit Lions, wishes three University of Texas footballers good luck. They are just before their Cotton Bowl clash with

Tennessee on January 1, 1950, after Texas took its first workout at S.M.U. upon arriving in Dallas, Texas, December 29, from Austin. Texas players left to right are: all-America Don Menasco, end Ben Proctor, and all-America guard Lewis (Bud) McFadin.

"It was soul-satisfying to wind up as coach of a champion in December after hearing the wolves howl well into October," Cherry said.

Cherry was a success all of his days in the coaching ranks from the glory years of the state's schoolboy power, the Amarillo Sandies, to the SWC football throne room. He died at Lubbock, Texas, in 1966 not many days after he had been told he had been selected to the Texas Sports Hall of Fame. Poor health certainly contributed to Cherry's resignation, but he was to say later he was unable to "relax under the constant strain of bigtime football."

It was under Cherry that Texas switched from Bible's wingback formation to the Chicago Bear T. With the help of Price as an assistant, Bobby Layne made the change from tailback to T quarterback and became one of the greatest the game has known.

Cherry chaffed under some alumni muttering behind his back, "Cherry can't win the close ones."

He said at a big school like Texas "someone is always gunning for you...if it isn't a disgruntled fan, it's the opposition...fair-weather followers are extremely sensitive to scores and victory margins—especially those dead-game sports who give twenty points and drop a couple of bucks."

Cherry decided to quit after the Longhorns had defeated SMU 23-20 in 1950—the same Mustang team that had earlier conquered the nation's No. 1 team, Ohio State.

He told Price he would recommend him for the job and made the announcement. The next week Bobby Dillon returned a punt eight-four yards in the last quarter to beat Baylor 20-17.

Texas lost in the Cotton Bowl to Tennessee, and Cherry turned the reins over to Price, saying "I'm going into the oil business which is simpler than football coaching. You dig a hole, and oil comes out or it doesn't."

Houston Chronicle columnist Dick Peebles said that Price was inheriting "one of the hottest football spots of any coach in the land. Here's hoping he has asbestos britches."

Price started quickly, coaching the 'Horns to the 1952 SWC championship and tying Rice for the championship in 1953, defeating Tennessee 16-0 in the 1953 Cotton Bowl game.

Texas slipped to fifth in 1954, and here came the mail and

Who says practice is a drag? Some Texas footballers back when they still played the game on grass.

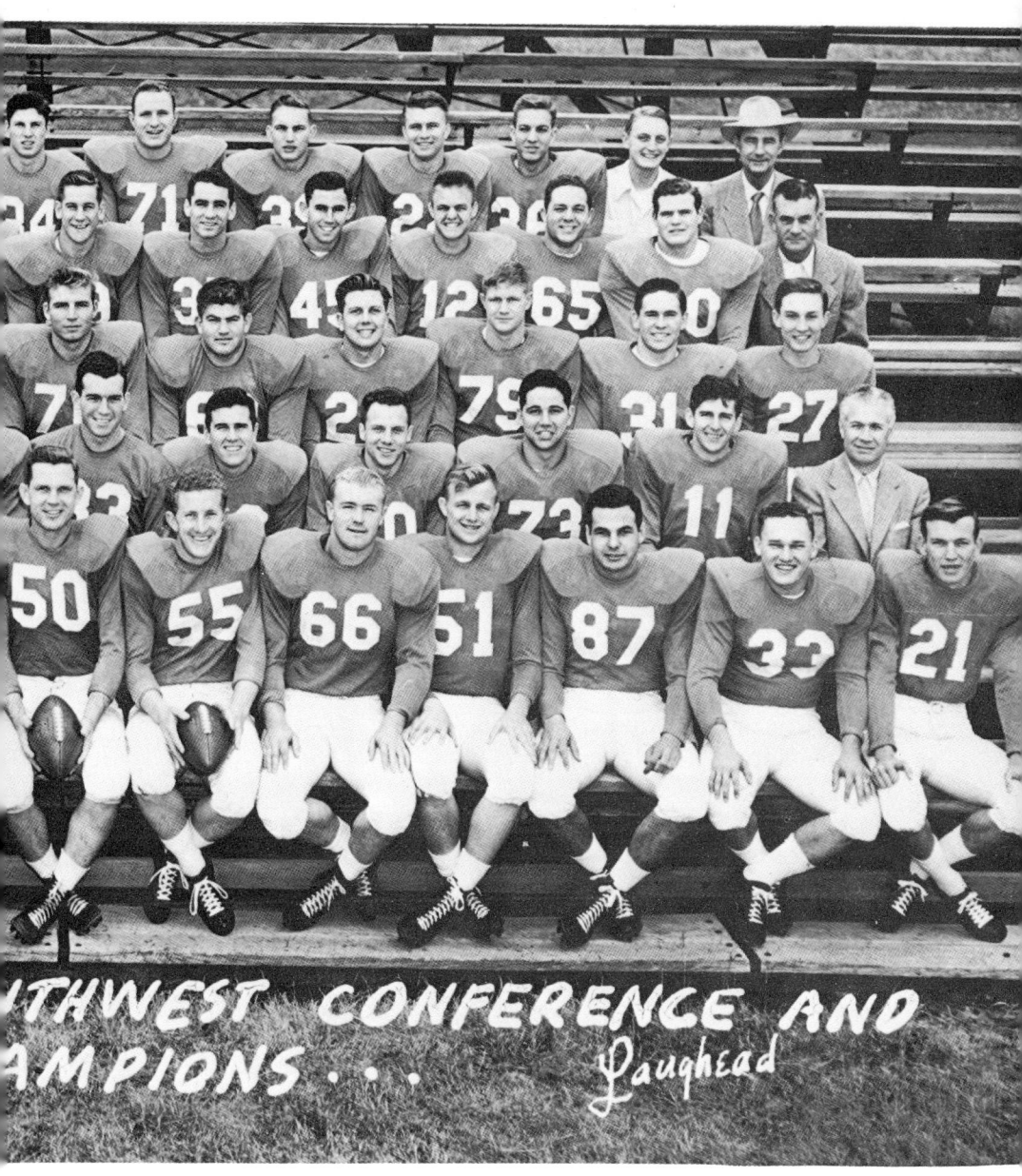

The Gib Dawson and Dick Ochoa bunch of 1952. Cotton Bowl and Southwest Conference champions.

the telephone calls. Price accepted the criticism much quieter than Cherry.

He said, "I don't mind the suggestions. Anyone who'll take the trouble to sit down and write what he believes could help the team, still has its interest at heart. People who do that are still behind you."

Price resigned in 1956 in the middle of what turned out to be a disastrous 1-9 campaign. Price's resignation was typical of him, hoping to unite the shattered alumni.

"When dissatisfaction and bitterness develop because of a losing season, no one profits," he wrote. "It is unfair to the team for us to have a house divided. These boys are entitled to the full support of the alumni. I don't want to stand in the way of that undivided support.

"Further, I do not want to put my friends on the spot. A great many people have assured me of their continued confidence and support...the harsh fact still remains, however, that under present conditions it is unlikely that all groups in the university circle can pull together. The Longhorns need just that."

His resignation was effective December 31, 1956.

Texas abandoned its policy of going with homegrown products after that and found Darrell Royal.

And where Cherry and Price ultimately found frustration, Royal was later to say, "I didn't expect all that has happened here...you dream and you hope, but what's happened is a little bit beyond my dreams."

The Royal Reign

In his office Darrell Royal has a painting of an old, scraggly range steer. The Longhorn has ribs showing, an ugly look in his eyes, and head slightly lowered set for a charge at the slightest provocation. The beast is obviously in search of a meal, and you get the feeling the Longhorn would not be picky about what he found.

Royal claimed that old discarded, dusty picture when he came to Texas in 1957. It says a lot about his philosophy.

"I'm fond of that painting," Royal says. "I don't want any fenced in, fat Longhorns around here. Just look at him. He doesn't know where his next meal is coming from. He's hungry, and he's not afraid to kick up a little dust. That's the way I want my football teams."

Royal himself went through more trials than a range Longhorn before he made himself a home at Texas and started a legend. The forty-nine year old Royal was one of six children in a Hollis, Oklahoma, family during the dread Dust Bowl days of the depression. His mother died when he was six. The dust was so bad he slept with a wet dishrag over his face.

Royal grew up with the taunting call of "Okie" haunting his every step. To this day he admits being sensitive about what people say.

"I've never denied being thin-skinned, and I think other people are too," Royal says. "I try to keep from saying anything that's not right or will hurt someone's feelings."

His father, Burley Royal, drove a gas truck for a farmer's

Darrell Royal in grade school at Hollis, Oklahoma.

co-op in the day and was a night watchman in the evenings. Highway 62 fronted his home in Hollis, and he used to stand and watch the flight to California in the early 1930s.

"I remember watching the cars and trucks go by with people jammed in and water jugs banging the sides—all heading West," Royal says.

Royal and his family joined the flight but he could not stomach California.

"I wasn't happy," Royal recalls. "Being called an 'Okie'

DKR decades later with a dynasty in his sights at Texas.

was something that, at that time, wasn't popular; it hurt."

Royal, with his father's permission, hitchhiked back to Hollis. He washed cars and shined shoes. Royal quarterbacked the Hollis team to an unbeaten season his senior year and found time to court Edith in between work, school, and football.

"Darrell didn't have a car, so we would walk down to the square on Saturday night near the jail and talk to the prisoners," Edith recalls.

"Yeh, we'd ask 'em what they were in for, and they'd ask

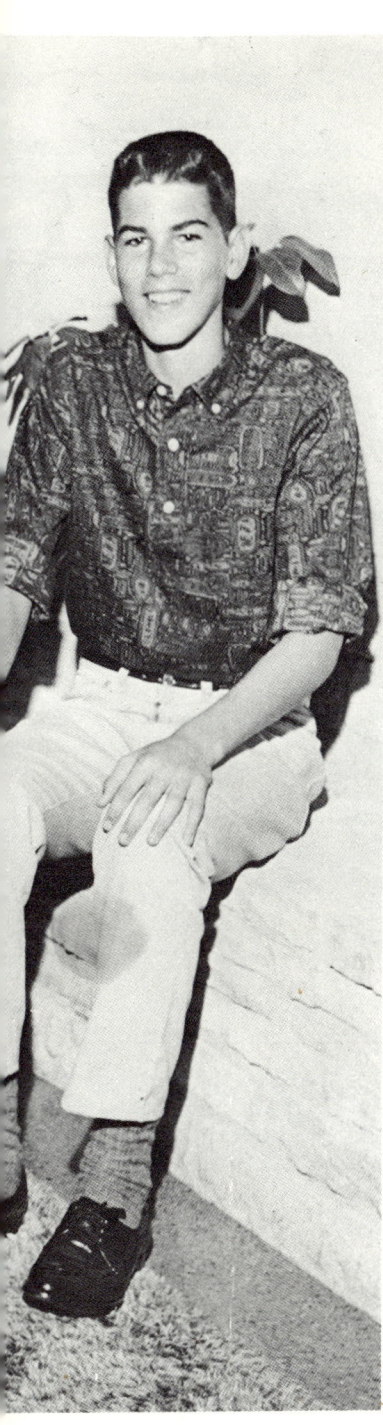

Darrell and Edith in a 1961 family portrait.

The price of victory sometimes comes in torn jersies. Witness 1961 quarterback Mike Cotton's wardrobe.

us how was it on the outside," Royal says.

Royal was a star back at Oklahoma from 1946-1949 under Bud Wilkinson after a stint in the Air Force during World War II. He began his coaching career as an assistant at North Carolina State in 1950 and served as an aide at Tulsa and Mississippi State. In 1953 he took over as head coach at Edmonton in the Canadian Professional League.

Mississippi State offered DKR his first head coaching job, and he compiled identical 6-4 seasons in 1954 and 1955. He spent a 5-5 year at Washington before a telephone call reached him one day after the 1956 season. It was the legendary Coach D.

X. Bible on the line. Bible was the UT athletic director, and the hunt was on for a replacement to Ed Price who had just finished with a 1-9 season.

"As you might expect, we had a lot of help in selecting a football coach," Bible recalled recently. "Bobby Dodd, who was at Georgia Tech, recommended that we telephone Darrell. I met him at the airport, and Darrell immediately wanted to know the people he was going to meet. I mean he wanted their first and last names."

Bibles says, "Members of the athletic council would ask him a question, and Darrell would reply, 'Well, Dean Burdine or Dr. Williams...needless to say it made quite an impression. I know it impressed me."

Royal was hired as head coach with the stipulation that he also become athletic director in five years.

"I stayed on in a consulting role," Bible says. "Darrell had a lot of energy. He came over frequently to talk."

One of the things Coach Bible emphasized to Royal was intense recruiting of kids inside the state.

"We needed to have more recruiting of boys inside the state, and it was important to keep a clean program," Bible says. "What a fine job Darrell has done."

Royal's first Texas team went 6-4-1, and he has never had a losing season in Austin.

Mike Campbell, Texas' defensive coordinator who has been Royal's right-hand man, gives this insight into what motivates his hardworking boss:

"The more he loses, the more fiercely he competes. But he is a gracious winner...if he had his right arm cut off, I believe he'd figure out a way that the thing was a hindrance to him—that he's better off with his left arm."

Campbell says Royal is more than fair with his players.

"He'll put down a big star," Campbell says. "He's never coddled any great player we've ever had. Darrell will get on the stars harder than on the other players."

Texas Sports Information Director Jones Ramsey says Royal is a little "I" and a big "We" man.

Royal, with his head set jammed to his ears, licking his fingers and hitching his pants, took the Longhorns to the Sugar Bowl in 1957 and suffered a shocking 39-7 loss to Mississippi.

To this day Royal considers it one of his biggest coaching embarrassments.

"We really shouldn't have gone there with that team," Royal says. "I did learn one thing from that game—to be a philosopher...that you are going to have your peaks and valleys. The secret to a successful career is to think you are going to eliminate the valleys and try not to get too concerned about any one big event overall."

Royal came back with a 7-3 record in 1958 and a 15-14 victory over Oklahoma that snapped a six-game Sooner win streak over the 'Horns. Texas was to win the next eight games from the hated Red River rivals.

The victory over Wilkinson's Sooners sent Longhorn fans into a frenzy.

"You've got to beat Oklahoma to get to stay around here," Bible says.

The Longhorns marched into the Cotton Bowl in 1959 for the first time under Royal and lost a bitter 23-14 decision to Syracuse. Some of the Syracuse players leveled charges of racism and dirty play against the Longhorn players. Royal invited one and all to view films of the game and make their own decision.

Royal, ever the innovator, put in the "flip-flop" offense in 1961 to make use of James Saxton, a leaf-in-the-wind type runner and one of the most exciting long-distance threats in Texas history. Saxton was moved from wingback to tailback, and the flip-flop switched the linemen so that the same people were always on the strong side.

Texas scored a sweet 12-7 victory over Mississippi in the 1963 Cotton Bowl.

Royal had proved he could win the big game, and one of the biggest of them all was just around the corner.

Getting Navy's Goat

To hear people from the East tell it, the unbeaten 1963 Texas team which was ranked No. 1 in the final AP and UPI polls could not have finished in the Ivy League's first division.

"Texas is the biggest fraud ever perpetrated on the football public," was one of the nicer jibes as once-beaten Navy and all-American quarterback Roger Staubach arrived in Dallas for the Cotton Bowl Classic.

Navy Coach Wayne Hardin openly challenged the Longhorns in the pregame introductions on national television, saying: "When the challenger meets the champion and the challenger wins, then there's a new champion."

Royal replied, "We're ready."

And were they ever. Hardin's navel would have jumped into his mouth if he had known at the very moment he made his statement Texas assistants were rehearsing their final plans around Navy defensive signals which had been detected on exchanged game films.

Royal explains how Texas stole Navy's defensive signals. "We had heard that the guy, (defensive coach), was pretty much out in the open," Royal recalls. "This guy gave his signals and didn't try to conceal or hide them like a baseball coach would do.

"We swapped all of our game film with them, and many times the Navy bench was across the field from the press box. When they shot the down box, many times you'd see that guy standing there giving a signal. Just looking at the film, if you

Duke Carlisle pitching and Phil Harris about to flee 63-yards for a touchdown with the tipped ball over Navy's Pat Donnely in the 28-6 Cotton Bowl victory January 1, 1964, to clinch the national title.

could spot him you could tell what defense they were going to be in the next play."

Royal continues, "We trained two ways. We trained if we got the signal and if it was correct information and how we would use it and if we didn't have the locks on them.

"We started out the football game not trying to steal the signals but looking and verifying that we did have them. After we once had them, we flashed the information to (quarterback) Duke Carlisle before he went into the huddle. He called the defense, the stunt...and then the play we were going to run."

Phil Harris beat Navy defensive back Pat Donnelly twice on touchdown bombs of 58 and 63 yards from Carlisle as Texas stormed to a 28-6 victory, leaving no question as to the national champion.

"We completed five passes when Navy had stunts called to the areas they vacated," Royal says.

Hardin admitted, "I've never seen a team that deserved to be No. 1 more than Texas."

The American Football Coaches Association later selected Royal as Coach of the Year. He had reached a plateau among the coaching elite in the nation.

Tommy Ford—considered one of the best clutch runners in Southwest Conference history. He was a tailback on the 1963 national championship team and capped a great career with a 26-yard gallop against Navy in the 1964 Cotton Bowl. Above he is following crisp blocking for a touchdown against Rice.

Leaves In The Wind

Jackie Crain...James Saxton...Chris Gilbert...leaves in the wind. Given a timely block, the trio represents instant touchdown. They gave Longhorn football fans and foes alike a goose pimple a step.

Little Cowboy Jack is responsible for a play that his old coach, D. X. Bible, often recalls as "The minute I'd like to best live over, but it actually required only fifteen seconds."

It was 1939, and Texas was struggling to get its football program on a firm foundation. Arkansas led 13-7 with a minute to play, and the Longhorns, with possession on their 31-yard line, were apparently doomed.

Crain took a short pass in the right flat and dodged tacklers like a young rabbit in expressway traffic on a 69-yard touchdown play. He then calmly kicked the winning extra point.

"That game proved Texas could be a winner, and it was all Jack's doing," says Bible. "He was a threat to go all the way each time he touched the ball."

Crain had rambled fifty yards for a touchdown earlier in the memorable game to keep Texas in the contest.

Asked once to explain his incredible knack for smelling out tacklers Crain replied, "Maybe I have a sixth sense...but for sure I know I have split vision. I could spot the color of uniforms far to the left or to the right, and if they weren't Orange and White I would stay out of the way."

While Crain was a cottontail rabbit with a sixth sense, Saxton

Jackie Crain, the sweet-running No. 33, when Texas showed signs of awakening as a football giant.

James Saxton whirls away on a touchdown run against Southern Methodist.

was a darting hummingbird. Saxton was so sensational he caused Coach Darrell Royal to remark: "James pulled us out of so many tough situations...why, you take a look at the Oklahoma game (of 1961) and you'd think his mother put it (the game film) together."

Royal said James is "like a balloon let go after blowing it up real tight...when he saddles up, he seems to ride off in all directions."

The all-America Saxton averaged 8.3 yards per carry his senior year and had season touchdown runs of 80, 79, 66, 56, 49, and 45 yards as Texas went on to whip Ole Miss 12-7 in the Cotton Bowl.

Crain, who saw Saxton play, said, "He can change directions so fast that the tacklers can't react to him."

Saxton weighed 164 pounds in college ball, while Nocona Jack Crain tipped the scales at 146.

"I thought I was too light for college football, but Coach Royal told me: 'James, we'll give you a chance to prove yourself.'"

Scrawny of frame, Saxton did just that. Saxton, who used to run down rabbits, said he developed his wild style of running because, "A small man has to find a way to protect himself. I've never been hit solid very often."

Royal added, "Saxton made a tackler look like he wasn't sincere about his job."

They called him "The Lizard" and ole No. 25, Chris Gilbert, found more than one crack in a defensive line to slither for three 1,000 yard plus seasons in his career in the late 1960s. Gilbert had the uncanny balance of a high-wire walker.

Royal once described Gilbert's running style by saying: "Did you ever try to drop a cat on his back? If you have, you know it can't be done. Chris is the same way. I bet if you'd hold his arms and legs and let him go from about three feet off the ground, he'd light running."

While Crain and Saxton made their runs from power sweeps, Gilbert ran from both the I and winged-T formations. Gilbert had a sprinter's speed out of the blocks, and when he reached the line of scrimmage was operating on all cylinders.

A cool customer, Gilbert was almost so relaxed before a game he could nod off. Afterwards he says, "I'd just stare at the

Chris Gilbert, the first runner in NCAA history to gain 1,000 yards in three consecutive seasons.

ceiling and replay the game until 3:00 a.m."

Royal said Gilbert was one of the "most talented and exciting runners who have been around."

Gilbert was mostly a north-south runner but could be knocked off balance and still come up running.

He was the first runner in NCAA history to gain 1,000 yards in three consecutive seasons. In the end he had a career total of 3,298 yards.

Crain, Saxton, Gilbert—yeh, what if they had played in the same backfield...

Coach Campbell

Mike Campbell, who has the bark of a Marine Corps sergeant and the bite of a toothless grandma, is that "other" head coach in Austin, Texas. He runs the Longhorn defense with an iron hand and a chaw of Red Man chewing tobacco the size of your fist jammed in his jaw.

Darrell Royal has always had good judgment, and he had judged Campbell the best defensive coach in the nation. No opponent will disagree, because under Campbell the Texas defense has been respected on equal footing with the Wishbone-T offense.

Campbell, one of the highest paid assistants in America with over $25,000 a year income, has turned down numerous head coaching offers to stay with Royal. He joined Royal at the University of Washington in 1956 and moved with him to Texas in 1957.

Royal has said of Campbell, "It means a lot to a coach when he can have confidence in a guy to just go off and run your defense. Mike's chock-full of basic horse sense and has saved us from making bad mistakes a hundred times."

Asked how much responsibility Campbell has in the Texas defensive scheme, Royal says, "Just 150 percent...like he was a head coach."

Campbell is perhaps the most colorful assistant coach in the United States and has carved himself a niche in Longhorn football history. He drives his players like a trail boss trying to make Dodge City with his cattle while the price is still high. He

Mike Campbell, defensive general of the Longhorn team, is Darrell Royal's trusted assistant. He is the highest paid assistant in University of Texas history. Campbell's sons have played football for Texas, and here he is shown with one Longhorn son.

storms, he fusses, he cusses. Campbell sends great streams of Red Man spewing into the air like a Yellowstone geyser.

His remarks are tinged with humor.

Campbell hates passing quarterbacks and has fumed more than once: "They ought to let the air out of the ball and make 'em play between the hash marks."

Campbell calls the defensive signals from the sidelines like a baseball third-base coach.

"He's a great student of the opponent," Royal says. "Mike is successful because he has an outstanding football mind. He likes to stay with the basics like me to cut things down to where you don't have confusion."

Texas defensive back Tommy Keel once gave this description of Campbell: "He uses a lot of strong language and reminds me of an old general...sort of a skinny Patton. He calls you 'son' in a folksy manner and appeals to your manhood. He's always talking about courage...one on one...seeing if you can whip the other guy. On the practice field he's a hard man...you can't be friends with him. But his technique is effective. He gets a lot of effort out of us."

Keel continues, "Sometimes I think he just has a crusty exterior...more or less puts up a front. It's the darndest thing. During practice you never see him smile...he's loud and harsh. But during a game he's relaxed, composed, and FRIENDLY. He's actually friendly on the sidelines and doesn't yell at all."

Royal says, "Mike's a little hard on the players sometimes, but he has the touch of knowing when to pull up—he's a fair person. He plays no favorites. That's a big thing in earning an athlete's respect."

Campbell has had sons Mike and Tom play under him. Tom intercepted a key pass in Texas' 21-17 victory over Notre Dame in the 1970 Cotton Bowl which gave the Longhorns the national championship. Texas publicist Jones Ramsey recalls that it is a good thing Campbell's wife, Mary, never saw how her boys were treated by their father.

"If Mary Campbell had ever come to practice, she would have divorced him because he was worse on them than anyone," Ramsey says.

In Campbell's tenure at Texas, he has turned out five all-Americans. To this day former players drop by to pay their regards.

Campbell looked up from practice one day to see Dan Mauldin, the hero of the 1965 Orange Bowl victory over Alabama, on the sidelines.

Ramsey, who was passing by, said, "What are you doing at practice, Dan?"

"Oh, I just like to watch Coach Campbell coach...of all my professors at the University of Texas, he knew his field better than they knew their's."

Campbell is not beyond playing practical jokes on his colleagues. Once he gave Assistant Athletic Director Bill Ellington a sack-full of one-liners for a speech in Brady, Texas. Ellington was loaded with Campbell-fed jokes when he landed at the Brady airport.

Ellington asked the man who greeted him what the format would be at the banquet. The guy replied, "Oh, nothing to it...you just talk ten or fifteen minutes...Mike Campbell was down here last year and told some of the greatest jokes you ever heard."

Ellington would not speak to Campbell for a week.

Campbell was a B-24 pilot in World War II and occasionally flies a private plane on recruiting visits. Royal remembers that Campbell had to land once at a small West Texas airport in a fifty-mile-an-hour crosswind.

"It got hairy, but Mike enjoys life so much I'd fly anyplace with him...anytime Campbell gets killed in a plane crash it'll be the plane's fault."

About the only thing people do not like about Campbell is his tobacco-chewing habits.

"You can see little brown splotches in the artificial turf sometimes even after they hoover it down," says one player. "You sure hate getting tackled there."

Ramsey says there is still a janitor in the University of Texas athletic offices who has a score to settle with Campbell. Campbell spit a big plug of Red Man into a coffee cup one Sunday and left it in a wastebasket. The janitor emptied the basket and got the juice on his arm.

"You could hear him cussin' up a storm," Ramsey remembers. "The janitor would have made us a helluva linebacker that day."

At Texas, Mike Campbell will motivate you one way or the other.

Big Red

Tommy Nobis was the subject that late October day after a Texas victory and someone asked Longhorn defensive coach Mike Campbell how "Booger Red" had performed in Campbell's often-critical eyes.

"Great, just great," Campbell said.

"How do you know Nobis played a great game without seeing the movies?" someone asked.

"Because he always plays a great game," Campbell shot back.

In eighty-one years of Texas football, six-foot-three, 230-pound Nobis may have been the very best of the defenders.

His size twenty-inch neck carried a helmet that looked like a torpedo tip. A ballcarrier crumpled from his tackles as though the enemy back had wandered into a load of No. 2 high-velocity chilled shot.

Pat Culpepper, a former Texas linebacker, said once, "When I'd tackle people they'd want to get up and get that so-and-so. With Tommy they'd just kind of stagger back to the huddle."

Nobis, a freckle-faced star of the early 1960s, left a legend that surpasses even the mightiest of Texas defensive stars like Malcolm Kutner, Tom Stolhandske, Scott Appleton, Don and Diron Talbert, Stan Mauldin, Bobby Dillon, Hub Bechtol, Carlton Massey, Harley Sewell, Grover Emerson, Claude Blanton, and others.

Although a vicious tackler, No. 60 was a quiet gentle man

Smokey the Cannon belches after a Texas touchdown. In the background you can see Big Bertha, the world's largest drum.

off the field.

"I don't know how hard I hit or anything, but it's the only way I can make the team," Nobis once said.

Nobis was so dedicated to football at Texas that he did not even mind the grind of the spring scrimmages.

"I surely don't dislike spring football," he once said. "I feel spring training is necessary, and it sure does help your timing."

Nobis may have been the best two-way lineman in Texas history. Darrell Royal said he was the best he ever coached. In one game in 1965, Nobis blocks paved the way for two touchdowns, he made twenty tackles, and intercepted a pass.

The San Antonio kid proved that he was not a college fluke in the pros. He made the all-Pro team at middle linebacker one year with Atlanta when the Falcons won a grand total of one game out of fourteen.

Asked the difference in playing for the Falcons and the Longhorns, Nobis says: "All through college football at Texas you have a winning tradition going for you. It makes it easy to get fired up for a game...the tradition is so important you would do anything to keep it.

"There wasn't a spring practice or a game week in my sophomore and junior year that I wasn't worried about losing my spot as a starter. Some guy awful good was always climbing right up my backside threatening to take over if I let up."

Nobis recalls he played in four straight losing games in his senior year at Texas but remembers, "I kept telling myself on every play to show some pride in the Orange and White."

The 1965 Orange Bowl game against Alabama was typical Nobis. He led a Longhorn charge which stopped the Joe Namath-led Crimson Tide four times inside the five-yard line to preserve a 21-17 victory.

"The only time I ever remember seeing Tommy really mad was after we had lost a game," recalls Culpepper.

"Pride is an important thing if you want to play football," Nobis says. "If you have any pride, you want to play the team that whipped you again the next day."

Whether he was lined up as a strongside guard on offense or a middle linebacker on defense, Nobis always gave Texas fans something to be proud of.

Royal And Recruiting

Although the fiercest of competitors in the schoolboy football star signing jousts, Royal has managed the Longhorn program without scandal. He will not cotton wrongdoing. Royal has gone so far as to suggest that recruiters be liable for polygraph tests if there is any question as to whether they have offered a high school prospect any incentive outside the NCAA boundaries.

"I'd hate to say we've deteriorated to the point where everyone should have to take a polygraph test, but I would be willing to do it," Royal says. "There should be some kind of a test that we could put people to. It might not be a bad idea. Say an investigator could get everything on Texas he was suspicious of and give it to an interrogator, and let him level off on those points.

"I tell you what, it could be pretty strong. The test would have to be given, not assuming that you are innocent but assuming you are guilty."

Royal says every year after recruiting he is "wrung out. In the latter stages it just goes on...and on...and on..."

Royal says that families of recruits who initially are looking forward to the courting of their sons by the major collegiate football powers go from welcoming coaches with open arms to closing doors on them.

"At the end of recruiting they feel extremely put upon and that they've been under all kinds of pressure," Royal says. "They don't get people to leave them alone at the end."

Royal says you can take the most highly recruited prospect, and if he will follow some simple guidelines the experience will be less of a hassle.

"First of all, from the very start, schools that you are really interested in, tell them the very first contact," Royal says. "The longer you let a school stay around, the harder it becomes to say 'No.' You get attached to the recruiter...he's a friendly guy...you get more obligated and more involved. The easiest time to say no is the very first contact that is made. A lot of kids are thoughtful and don't want to hurt anyone's feelings."

Royal continues, "I honestly believe there are a very few kids that don't have a preference before school starts. If they just stick with those preferences that would eliminate a whole lot of it." Selecting a college has to be made by thousands of students all over the state of Texas. The families don't go through a major breakdown over children deciding where they are going to college...it's only the ones being recruited."

He adds, "If I had a child under recruitment, I wouldn't allow all that recruiting. I would insist on a maximum of three visits and get all that talking over with as quickly as possible. I've always tried to run a clean honest program, but the thing I resent the most is people saying: 'Royal doesn't have to cheat. He's at the University of Texas.' That's a helluva way to give a guy credit for not cheating. I really do accept that as an insult. I've coached at other schools, and we didn't fudge at recruiting, and I didn't have the recruiting advantage."

Royal says being successful in recruiting and on the football field can have its disadvantages.

"When we were riding high a couple of years back and had our back-to-back national championships and had defeated Oklahoma five or six times in a row...it got so the only ones who were really pulling for Texas were true orange bloods," Royal says. "That's just the nature of man...we pull for underdogs...I pull for underdogs...I like to see somebody else share a little of that wealth. The old saying that even your best friends don't like to see you too successful is true. Everybody likes to see a little wind taken out of your sails."

Royal says, "I think we reached the point that even in the state of Texas some of the people received a little satisfaction

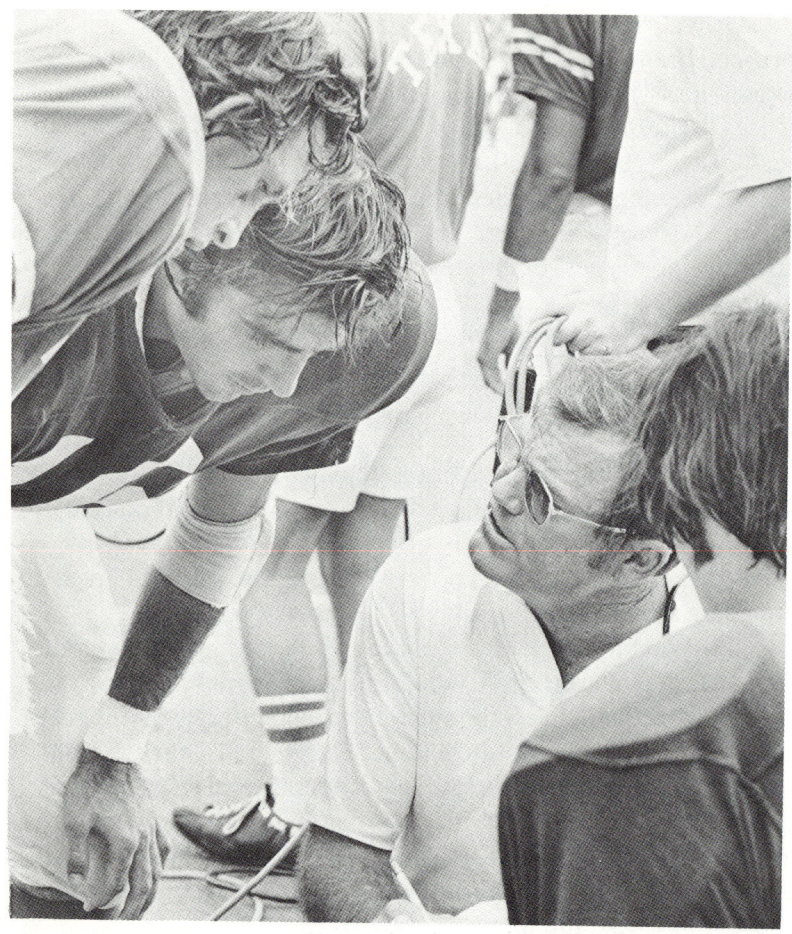

On the sidelines with Royal under the pressure-cooker of game tension. A place more to DKR's liking than the recruiting wars.

when Oklahoma defeated us the first time. They received less satisfaction the second time. And now we might even have a few Baylor types and a few Aggies pulling for us when we play Oklahoma because that old state pride starts coming back."

Royal says the best recruiting years are after the Southwest Conference has lost to teams with prospects recruited out of the state of Texas.

"It just takes a small dose of that to get everybody's attention," Royal says. "State pride starts coming back up again. The orange bloods are always going to be for you."

But he adds, "So much of public opinion is reflected by the sportswriters. I think even a lot of Texas writers were pulling for Oklahoma. You know, not just jumping up and down and pounding the counter when Oklahoma was doing well, but it really didn't bother them."

"Now I think some of the writers like seeing us getting that bronze hat (awarded to the winner of the Oklahoma-Texas game) back down here. They (the writers) really didn't care three years ago."

Royal believes in recruiting kids from Texas because of the state pride factor. Only seldom will he go out of the state to brand a Jim Bertelsen, a tremendous running back from Green Bay, Wisconsin, who now stars for the Los Angeles Rams.

He makes three demands of his recruits: "That he be ambitious in his studies and make proper progress toward graduation; that he conduct himself like a gentleman and reflect credit on the university; and, that he be a competitor."

Royal promises never again to make the same mistake he did after the Cotton Bowl victory over Navy in 1964 which cemented the national title.

"I ran all over the country receiving honors and awards because I was in demand," Royal recalls. "I didn't spend enough time recruiting, and my record really suffered. I had three 6-4 seasons back-to-back."

Royal has recruited with vigor since.

The Birth Of The Wishbone

You would think that after Darrell Royal had won a national title in 1963, there would be little question about his talent as a head coach. But there were some doubting orange bloods after three consecutive four-loss years from 1965-1967.

There was a satisfying 21-17 Orange Bowl victory over Alabama and Joe Namath in January, 1965. But then Texas went 6-4, 7-4, and 6-4.

It was a restless summer of 1968 for Royal. He was pondering the use of a triple-option attack amid growing concern by his doubters that he was falling behind the times offensively.

"It was a shaky time," Royal recalls. "A lot of people were beginning to question me. You know...they'd say football had kind of bypassed me...I was stubborn...everybody had gone to two split receivers and a pro set, and here we had reverted to a fullhouse backfield...probably the only team in the country. A lot of people were saying 'Well, maybe he was just a flash in the pan, and he can't repeat it.'"

What transpired that summer and fall was the birth of the Wishbone-T offense—an attack that revolutionized collegiate football into a high-scoring, crowd-pleasing game. A high school coach, an idea by assistant Emory Bellard...then Texas A&M head coach Gene Stallings, the Houston Veer...all figured prominently in Royal's decision to go to the fullhouse backfield.

Royal says that Bellard, now head coach at Texas A&M

University, had the basic idea of the alignment now used by hundreds of collegiate teams across the country, but it was a high school coach who was ahead of the times. "The first time I remember seeing what we are running was when Gene Henderson was coaching at Nederland, Texas, High School," Royal recalls. "They were running a triple option on the theory developed first at the University of Houston, but they were running it from the I-formation, faking to the fullback just like we do with the tailback set behind him and he was the pitch man.

"So, the idea of a fullback being the handoff man both to the right side and the left side was at Nederland High School. My first time to see it was on film. We got on the blackboard and talked about it."

Royal says the first time he saw it run in college was at Texas A&M under Stallings, a former assistant to Paul (Bear) Bryant of Alabama, and later an assistant for the Dallas Cowboys of the National Football League.

"They had the fullback up very tight," Royal remembers. "That's the year (1967) they go on to the Cotton Bowl and beat Alabama. They had Wendell Housley at fullback. The thing we feared most about our game with Texas A&M that year was this offense. It gave us a lot of concern, but they only used it a few times in the ball game (won by the Aggies 10-7)."

Royal says, "I just wasn't happy with our offense, and Emory wanted to run the triple option, and he had done some study on it. The idea of faking the handoff to the fullback had already been used a little bit. I said whatever offense we change to, we've got to have a fullhouse backfield because we had Chris Gilbert, Ted Coy, and Steve Worster. I thought they were all good enough running backs to be in the same backfield."

Texas unveiled the Wishbone (which still did not have a name) against Houston in the season opener September 21, 1968. The Longhorns had the fullback up close to the quarterback like A&M had done against Alabama on New Year's Day. The game ended in a 20-20 deadlock with "Super" Bill Bradley at quarterback.

Royal later moved the fullback two steps back and instead of having the tailback stacked right behind the fullback, he split the backs.

Texas has long lived off its defense. Here is an excellent example, as a lineman returns an intercepted pass.

"Emory came up with the idea of the Wishbone as we line up in it today," Royal says. "There were many things we had been running that made it acceptable to me. We had been running the inside belly which I got from (Arkansas Coach) Frank Broyles when he was at Georgia Tech and I was at Mississippi State. That was the first time I ever got the inside belly...the second man through.

"Now, we've made some refinements and changes in the inside belly, but still it's basically the same play...just one or two little ole changes. We got that from Frank Broyles."

In the next game against Texas Tech, Royal had to replace Bradley at quarterback with untested, but gritty, James Street, a junior. Texas lost to Texas Tech, and Oklahoma State loomed ahead the next weekend. Royal had made a crucial decision about a formation. Now he had to make one about his quarterback situation.

"It was the hardest decision I had to make," Royal says. "To tell a great athlete, Bill Bradley, that we were moving him to defense. That was really hard because Bill had a world of pride, and tremendous ability. I do not think his ability called for him to be playing at quarterback. He probably feels hurt to this day, but it was a decision I had to make, and he was too good a football player to sit on the bench. I wanted it to be cleanly and clearly decided who was quarterback. I didn't want to have that thing shuffling back and forth."

The Oklahoma State contest—the third game of the 1968 season—was termed by Royal as one of the most crucial in his coaching reign at Texas.

"A lot of people were down on us about that time," Royal says. "They said we got tied and defeated in the offense, and now we've switched quarterbacks. It was a shaky time. Before the Oklahoma State game I called on the student body, which is the only time I've done that in seventeen years at Texas. I asked them to rally behind the team. I worked at getting a pep rally up myself, which I've never done before or since, just to kind of get everything rekindled again. I think that Oklahoma State game was one of the most important and crucial that we've had in keeping our program alive."

Texas won nineteen consecutive games and a national title under Street. The Longhorns captured thirty victories in a row with the Wishbone before Notre Dame upset the 'Horns in the Cotton Bowl at the end of the 1970 season.

The Wishbone was the start of six consecutive trips to the Cotton Bowl for the 'Horns, who owned a 55-10 record with the offense going into the 1974 season.

Texas tromped Oklahoma State 31-3 and downed Oklahoma 26-20 on an 80-yard drive in the fading minutes the next week on heroics by Street and Worster.

Royal was discussing the "Y" formation with writers in 2001 of the Villa Capri the next week after a 39-29 victory over Arkansas when sportswriter Mickey Herskowitz of the *Houston Post* asked, "Why don't you call it the Wishbone-T, Coach?"

The name stuck, and the Longhorns became college football's most deadly team for the next five years. The National Collegiate Sports Service ranked Texas the No. 1 collegiate team in regular season play from 1968 through 1973 with a .910 percentage.

Since 1968 there has not been any talk of football bypassing Darrell Royal.

The beginning of a Wishbone play—a handoff or fake to the fullback—in this instance former Longhorn great Steve Worster.

Once In A Lifetime

"I don't think there can ever be another year like that...certainly not in my lifetime."

Sometimes Darrell Royal looks back on the events of the 1969 season and wonders if they really happened. It was a storybook year and will forever be etched in University of Texas archives as the most electrifying season in the rich Longhorn football history.

It was collegiate football's centennial year, and ABC-TV thought it would be a dandy idea if Texas and Arkansas put off their expected showdown for the Southwest Conference title until December. The odds were good both teams would be unbeaten, and it would be a grand climax to 100 years of college football right there on the "boob tube."

Royal and Arkansas coach Frank Broyles agreed on the October to December switch in dates. But they never dreamed what pressures lurked ahead on December 6, 1969, in Fayetteville, Arkansas, in a joust later to be billed as "The Game of the Century."

Texas, with James Street at the controls of the awesome Wishbone, mauled opponent after opponent. The Longhorns warmed up for the December date by crushing TCU 69-7, then battering Texas A&M 49-12. Arkansas cruised along unbeaten behind the passing of Bill Montgomery and the receiving of Chuck Dicus.

The buildup to the game bordered on hysteria.

"I don't think we'll ever have a buildup for a game like

122

A pep rally attended by 35,000 in Memorial Stadium before the 1969 victory over Arkansas.

that again," Royal says. "We were playing in December...we were ranked No. 1 (Texas) and No. 2 (Arkansas)...the President was there...we followed that up with a come-from-behind victory in the Cotton Bowl (over Notre Dame.) No, I don't think there can ever be another year like that. There's no way in

my lifetime I'll ever see a pep rally that attracts 30,000 to 35,000 people.

"I don't think I'll ever see the time where I had to remain aboard the airplane simply because I was afraid to get off. Normally you like to get out there and have people pat you on the back. That was so unsafe. The crowd was swirling. I was literally afraid to get off. They got me in a car, and we got clearance to drive on the runway through the back part. That was kind of strange to be driving in that squad car right out there on the ramp where the airplanes were going to be taking off and landing...I'd never done that before."

Texas defeated Arkansas 15-14 largely through the fourth

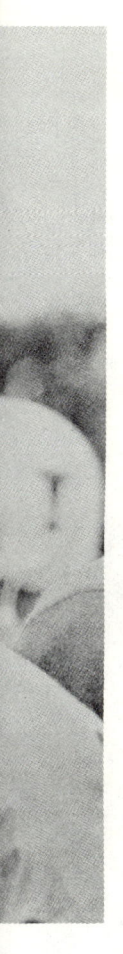

A grim Royal in the early going against Arkansas in Big Shootout I.

quarter heroics of Street, and President Nixon proclaimed the Longhorns the No. 1 team in the nation. The howls from unbeaten Penn State could be heard all the way from Pennsylvania.

Royal was later to allow that Texas was "lucky" to have beaten Arkansas, which led 14-0 going into the fourth quarter before Street ran 42 yards for a touchdown and worked his fourth down magic for a long bomb to Randy Peschel to set up the game clincher.

Royal judged that Arkansas was better prepared emotionally and technically. He thought the Razorbacks had outplayed his club.

Joy on the Texas bench in Big Shootout I against Arkansas for the national title.

"We had one great play, and we had a gutsy call, but the rest of it stunk," Royal concluded.

President Nixon declared in the locker room, "This was one of the greatest games of all time...the wire services will name Texas the No. 1 team, and this is a great honor in the one-hundredth year of college football. The fact that you won a tough game and the fact that you didn't lose your cool and

didn't quit makes you deserving of No. 1."

Royal knew that it was the "The Rat" or "Slick" as his teammates called him, who had kept his cool with the eyes of the nation watching.

Royal said: "James Street is a winner...and that's the nicest thing you can say about anybody."

The Fourth Down Phantom

Like a retired, undefeated gunfighter, James Street's legend grows. In the annals of University of Texas football there is no equal to Street's brinkmanship. He was the fourth down phantom, the gutsy little gambler with the confidence of a Las Vegas high roller.

He never lost a game he started at quarterback in nineteen contests through the 1968 and 1969 seasons that eventually earned Royal his second national championship. Street accomplished the impossible with an elan that follows him to this day at football banquets in Texas.

"Now, not only was I undefeated as a quarterback, but I never lost on the pitcher's mound either," Street says with a smile. "Bobby Layne was never beaten as a baseball pitcher. I got the heck kicked out of me at Omaha (site of the NCAA baseball playoffs) more than once."

Street faced prohibitive odds at Texas from the very moment he left Longview High School.

"A lot of recruiters told me that if I came to Texas I'd spend my career sitting on the bench behind Bill Bradley," Street remembers. "Coach Royal told me, 'James, if you start running from competition now you'll never know if you can compete.' That did it—I went to Texas."

Street's greatest distinction at Texas his freshman year was almost drowning in Lake Austin. A non-swimmer, Street was in a canoe rammed by Deryl Comer and Bob McKay.

"I had cracked ribs and couldn't swim, but I remember

clawing myself to the top of the water," Street says. "I had to swallow a lot of water before they were convinced I wasn't faking."

Street got the nickname "Rat" as in "drowned rat" from that episode. Later he was to be known as "Slick" because that is what he called most people: "Hey, Slick."

In 1968 Royal installed the Wishbone offense, and Street could be barely found on the depth chart. He was running behind Bradley and Joe Norwood. The Longview longshot was third-string and fading fast on the depth chart.

Texas and Houston tied 20-all in the opener, and the 'Horns trailed Texas Tech 28-6 in the third quarter the next week.

"James, get in there," Royal barked.

"I almost jumped out of the stadium," Street says. "I really don't think Coach Royal had all that much confidence in me. He was just looking for someone to send in."

Street performed remarkably although Texas lost 31-22—which was to be the last Longhorn defeat in thirty games.

"James is correct in saying I didn't have all that much confidence in him, but let me tell you he got my attention quick," Royal says.

Royal told Bradley before the next game that he was moving the heralded "Super Bill" to defense and installing Street as the regular quarterback.

"Bill had the greatest talent of any athlete I ever saw, but he was never what you call lucky," Street says. "I guess I'm probably the luckiest guy ever to play quarterback, particularly on fourth down. Bradley was a helluva lot better athlete than I was."

Street says he will never forget what class Bradley, a senior, showed in taking the demotion to defense. He called the team together and said, "Now, here's what we're going to do on defense. 'The Rat' will take care of the offense."

Texas' 31-3 victory over Oklahoma State with Street at the controls the next week set into motion what Royal calls one of the most important eras in his career.

The five-foot-eleven, 170-pound Street gave Longhorn fans a taste of what was in store against Oklahoma the next week.

Street sparked Texas on a last-minute 80-yard drive to conquer Oklahoma 26-20.

Asked what drove him, Street replied simply, "I like to beat people...I like to win."

Texas killed Tennessee 36-13 in the Cotton Bowl Classic to set the stage for the 1969 "Game of the Century" between the No. 1 ranked Longhorns and No. 2 rated Arkansas in Fayetteville the following December.

"The buildup for the game was incredible, but I still remember how cool Coach Royal was," Street says. "Here we were on a bus going to the game with all those Arkies yelling 'Soooiii-ee pig' and waving those doggone red banners, and Coach Royal was calmly discussing what play he wanted me to run if we had to go for two points. Danged if we didn't do it."

Texas fumbled the opening kickoff, and Arkansas scored two touchdowns and had a third called back. It was a rout and should have been worse than 14-0, Arkansas, going into the fourth quarter.

"You got to be lucky, but I just felt there was something I could do to turn things around," Street recalls.

Texas had second and nine to go on the Arkansas 42, and Street called a slant-in pass to tight end Randy Peschel over the center.

"I remember fading back and having trouble finding Randy," Street says. "I could feel pressure and decided to run. I just burst out of there, and their safety (Terry Stewart) slipped. I couldn't believe it. I was so scared I must have run that 40 in four seconds flat."

The touchdown cut Arkansas' lead to 14-6, and Street trotted off the field only to see Royal wave him back. Time for the two-pointer they discussed on the bench.

Street called "59 Base" in the huddle—an outside option. Street kept the ball and just made it over the goal to narrow the margin to 14-8.

Texas later scrambled back to the Longhorn 43, facing fourth and three with 4:47 left to play.

Royal, remembering that the Arkansas defensive backs had been coming up fast on Peschel, called '53 Veer Pass' as Street gaped in amazement during time out on the sidelines.

"I went back a second time to make sure that's what

James Street and Darrell Royal concoct the fourth down pass that helped win the "Game of the Century" in 1969 against Arkansas.

Coach Royal wanted," Street says. "I remember Coach Campbell calling the defense together and saying 'Now, we're going to give them the ball in our end of the field so we've got to stiffen up!...'"

Street says "I went back to the huddle and didn't look at Peschel when I called the play. Coach Royal doesn't know it to this day, but I gave Peschel a triple option. I told him if he thought he could get the three yards, stop, and beat his man, to do it. I told him if he thought he could get open by cutting to the sidelines to do it...and I told him if he thought he could beat his man deep to take off. I told the offensive line to give me time to read Randy. I think it was Bob McKay who said 'Yeh, block like it was a punt.'"

Street launched the ball and was whacked hard to the turf by the onrushing Razorback linemen. Peschel snared the perfectly thrown pass just over the outstretched fingers of two Arkansas defenders and sprawled out of bounds on the 13. Jim Bertlesen scored from three yards out, and Happy Feller kicked the winning extra point.

Street was hailed by the nation's press as a nervy "riverboat gambler," but he was to give an encore in the Cotton Bowl Classic as Notre Dame made its first bowl appearance in forty-five years.

The Longhorns came from behind to score with 1:08 left to defeat the Fighting Irish 21-17. Twice Street converted fourth downs on the drive—once at the Notre Dame 20 and the second time at the Irish 10. Facing fourth and two at the Irish

10, Street rolled left and threw a low pass to Cotton Speyer who made an acrobatic catch for a vital first down to set up the winning touchdown.

"I guess you could call it lucky that I threw the ball low and a little behind Cotton, but that's the way the ball had to be thrown to be completed...he was really covered," Street says.

Street, now in insurance, says, "It doesn't scare me to look back on those days. In both instances we just executed."

Once asked for a self-appraisal, Street said, "I'm not very big, I can't run fast, and I can't throw, but I can give you everything of what's left."

Street's legend is simply that he was a competitor.

"As good as any I ever saw," says Royal.

Street and Bobby Lane have often been compared as the most competitive quarterbacks in Texas history.

A teammate of Street once said: "I've never met Mr. Layne, but I've read about him all my life and the pep talks he used to give. Well, James kept you perked up. Sometimes he got so involved with firing us up in the huddle, he forgot to call the signals."

Never on fourth down!

James Street on the launching pad to Randy Peschel as Texas' greatest fourth down quarterback connects in the historic 1969 Arkansas game.

"A Game Ball For Freddie"

Just when Texas coach Darrell Royal was savoring the fruits of winning collegiate football's most celebrated game, he was brought to earth in late December, 1969, with the shattering news that his toy safety, Freddie Steinmark, had cancer.

"I was in New York accepting the MacArthur Bowl and riding on cloud nine when I got the telephone call," Royal recalls.

The stunned Royal, who had a special place in his heart for the 152-pound, 5-foot-10 scrapper from Wheatridge High School in Denver, could only sputter that Steinmark would fight his new opponent with the same courage he displayed on the football field.

"He's got a tubfull of guts—that's all I can say," Royal said.

Steinmark's leg was amputated days later. He bravely announced that he would be on the sidelines New Year's Day when Texas lined up against Notre Dame's Fighting Irish.

As the plucky Steinmark raced against time to gain control of his crutches, the Texas team quietly went about dedicating themselves to winning the game ball for Freddie. Before the game Royal recalled why he signed the skinny Colorado kid when others looked away.

"How could I be prejudiced against him?" Royal said. "I just weighed 158 pounds when I started out at Oklahoma. I suspicioned he (Steinmark) had 150 pounds of heart. My

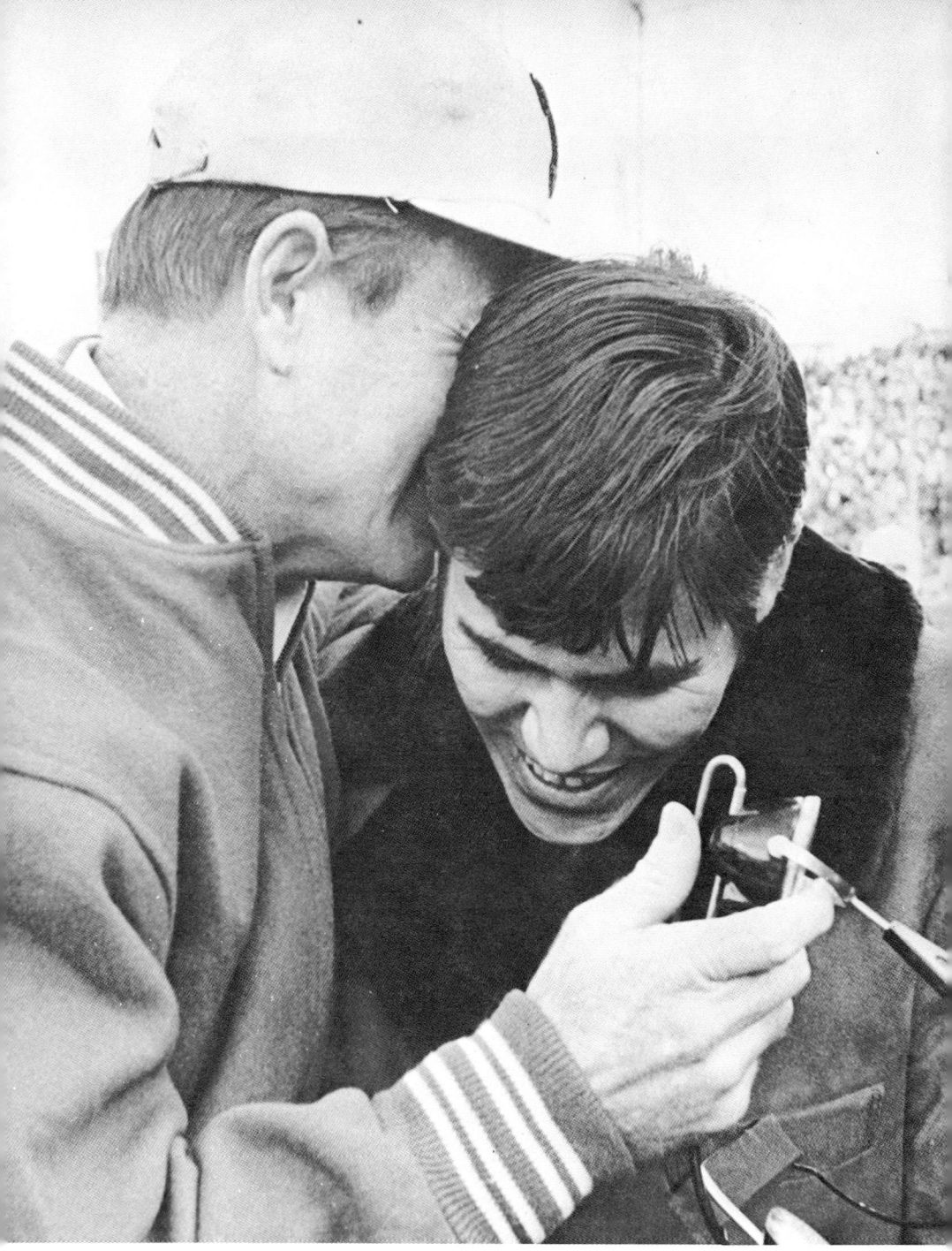

With the victory in the bag, Darrell Royal enjoys a private joke with tragedy-stricken Freddie Steinmark in the closing seconds of a 21-17 Cotton Bowl victory in 1970 over Notre Dame.

An "Orange Blood" giving DKR a pat on the cheek after the 1970 Cotton Bowl victory over Notre Dame.

suspicions were correct."

Steinmark somehow made it to the game and went to the dressing room briefly before he made his way to the sidelines.

"Freddie picked us all up with his appearance before the game," Ted Koy said later. "He didn't have to say anything. There was communication enough."

The Associated Press lead that day read:

DALLAS (AP)—Top-ranked Texas, its inspiration standing erect on crutches along the sideline, resorted to its fourth down magic twice Thursday and spoiled Notre Dame's first bowl appearance in forty-five years with a 21-17 Cotton Bowl victory.

"With shouts of 'Let's go, let's go, this one's for Freddie,' the Longhorns rallied from behind to score with 1:08 remaining to defeat the Fighting Irish and wrap up the national championship.

"Safety, Fred Steinmark, whose cancerous left leg was amputated several weeks ago, let out a loud yell along with the joyous Longhorn bench as Billy Dale plunged across from one yard out for the winning touchdown.

"Texas had dedicated the game to Steinmark, who was given the game ball. He accepted it with tears in his eyes."

For Royal and the team there was tremendous relief that they had not let Freddie down—a Catholic who dearly wanted to play against the Irish because they had not recruited him.

The post-game telephone call from President Nixon was anti-climactic.

"I thought you played like champions," Nixon said.

But all that really mattered to the Texas team was that Freddie Steinmark thought so.

Symbol Of Courage

At the age of twenty-one Freddie Steinmark was to shun accepting with bitterness the role fate had placed on him.

"You just have to be realistic and take what comes in life," Steinmark told the Philadelphia Sportswriters Association in accepting the Most Courageous Athlete of the Year award.

His faith was unshakeable, and he even made jokes about his condition. Told that some friends were going to write a book about him, Steinmark said, "It should be easy to read...it'll be things like 'See Fred. See Fred hop. Hop. Hop. Hop.'"

With the help of Catholic priest Father Fred Bomar, Steinmark progressed to the point where he could play nine holes of golf and once shot a creditable 46. He took up water skiing, and his balance was remarkable. Even under the ravages of cancer his athletic talent and attitude had not changed from the day Royal recruited him.

But the visits to M. D. Anderson Hospital and Tumor Institute in Houston became more frequent. On June 6, 1971, Steinmark died. His backfield coach Freddie Akers said, "Certainly he has been an inspiration to countless youngsters around the country. We'll never be prouder of anyone than we are of him."

Before he died Freddie wrote a book entitled, *I Play to Win*, with the aid and expertise of Blackie Sherrod, the executive sports editor of the *Dallas Times Herald*. Sherrod was one of the last persons to visit Freddie before he died. Sherrod wrote a column to be released on the day of Steinmark's death.

Headlined "Requiem for an all-American," the column is reprinted here with special permission:

Six months after they took the left leg of Freddie Steinmark, he returned to the Houston tumor clinic for another of his nervewracking checkups. The little Texas safety had to do this every three months, as do all victims of osteogenic sarcoma. He underwent blood tests and x-rays to determine if the dread maglignancy might appear in other parts of his strong young body.

For several nights preceding his trips to M. D. Anderson Hospital, Freddie would stare at the ceiling. He knew the odds. He prayed for a miracle.

"They told me not to worry, but that's easy for them to say," Freddie said. "They're the ones taking the x-rays, not the one getting them."

When Freddie would get a clean report, he would return joyously to the Texas campus and throw himself into another project with fierce energy. He took up golf, balancing himself on one leg while he swung. He learned to water ski. He went religiously to the Longhorn weight room to build up the rest of his body, as if muscle could hold off any return invasion of cancer cells. He worked his grades back to a B average. He made speeches and appearances. He wanted feverish activity to keep his mind occupied, so it wouldn't wander back to the calendar and the date of his next trip to Houston.

Last July a couple of blurs showed up on x-rays of Freddie's lungs. It could be one of several things, the doctors told Freddie, we'll watch it close. A bit later, they told Freddie he would have to start a series of chemotherapy treatments. He didn't change expressions. But he guarded the news as if it were the atomic secret. He wanted no one to know. It was almost as if Freddie thought the treatments were a sign of personal weakness. The news might bring pity from his teammates and friends and above all, he didn't want that.

The chemo-therapy consisted of six days of shots that, hopefully, would kill or arrest any fast-growing cancer cells. They make the patient frightfully nauseous.

Freddie Steinmark—ramrod stiff on the sidelines of the 1970 Cotton Bowl showdown with Notre Dame.

But he masked the trips and treatments from all save a precious few. Scott Henderson, the linebacker and Freddie's apartment mate, knew, but he respected the confidence.

One possible side effect of chemo-therapy shots is the loss of hair. Freddie had a long thick black mane, and he was proud of it. His teammates teasingly accused him of being a hippie. "Okay, you guys," he said. "I'm gonna help coach the freshmen defensive backs and just to show you how seriously I'm taking this job, I'll get rid of the hippie image. I'll get rid of all this hair. As a matter of fact, I'll just shave it all off, just to show you I'm not kidding."

So the Texas squad had a little ceremony in the locker room, and they all laughed and cheered as Bobby Wuensch shaved off the Steinmark hair. His teammates didn't realize he dreamed up this little act to hide the fact he was taking treatments that made his hair fall out. He kept his head shaved. Rick Troberman took note of the bald head and the missing leg and applied the nickname "Pirate." Freddie went along with the gag. He had his ear pierced and wore a gold ring in it for a while.

He shared his worry and concern with no one. But sometimes when you were in a conversation with Freddie, he would be staring at you vacantly with those enormous black eyes and there would be a silence, and he would say, "Excuse me, I guess I wasn't listening. What did you say?"

To the last, Freddie refused to accept the idea that the cancer had caught up with him and finally dragged him down. When he was hospitalized this last time in M. D. Anderson, he believed—at least outwardly—that he was there to have some fluid removed from his body. When his priest from Austin, Father Fred Bomar, walked quietly into Room 514W and sat down, Freddie looked at him narrowly.

"Have you got some business in Houston, Father?" he said. The priest said no, he just came down for a visit.

"Do you know something I don't know?" asked Freddie. The priest said no.

His friends thought it was rather a miracle, Freddie having played regularly on a national championship team with the tumor already gnawing at his leg, and had survived the amputation and returned to active life, had been able to move back into society, to tell people how he felt, to squeeze another 17 months out of precious life. Freddie didn't think it was a miracle; it was what an athlete was supposed to do and now that same fierce competition kept him hanging on for days, weeks, after the average person would have let go. Doctors walked out of his room with tears in their eyes.

Two weeks ago, I visited the room. The shades were drawn. A television set suspended from the ceiling, with the volume off, flickered lifelessly with a soap opera. There was a skinny couch with bed pillows along on one wall, where Freddie's mother, Gloria, and his girl friend, Linda Wheeler, spent each day and his father spent each night. A vigil candle on a table burned twenty-four hours a day. Freddie was a gaunt shadow and his voice was about gone and I had to bend close to hear him whisper, "I'm getting better."

Freddie has written a book about his experiences. It will be published this fall. The editor noticed after Freddie was hospitalized, that he had not made a dedication of the book and he asked to whom Freddie wanted to dedicate his story. Freddie said to the Lord, who had been so good to him.

Scribes And The Man

It was several summers ago, and Bob (Chickenfry) Galt visited with Darrell Royal in his small dressing room just off the coach's office. Royal was reminiscing to the sportswriter how times were changing. The Texas coach held up a can of hair spray and pointed to it.

"I'll tell you how things have changed...three years ago I would be hiding this," Royal said.

Perhaps Royal's success can be traced to the fact he has never fallen behind the times. He bends with the wind, and in most instances is a half-jump ahead of it.

Someone pointed out to Alabama Coach Paul (Bear) Bryant that Texas' 1969 national champion team had their hair showing under their helmets.

"If we could play like Texas, that'd be just fine with me too," said the usually straight-laced Bryant.

Once hard-rock defensive coach Mike Campbell came to Royal about the length of quarterback James Street's sideburns.

"Coach, James is letting his sideburns and hair get awful long. I guess we'd better have him cut it off..." or Campbell added with a wink, "Grow some hair of our own."

Texas sportswriters, who can be a rather penetrating group, have varying reasons why Royal has been an unprecedented success in a cannibalistic league where others have failed.

Burle Pettit, former executive sports editor of the *Lubbuck Avalanche-Journal* and now the managing editor, said of Royal: "He has a constant grasp of reality. You see people get

Royal takes time from a round of golf in a pro-am to greet some old friends in the gallery. He was playing with a guy named Arnold Palmer at the time. DKR plays golf to unwind from the tensions of big time football, and this particular scene is at the Byron Nelson Golf Classic in May in Dallas.

carried away on tangents, but with him everything seems to be right here. He's as real as the background he came out of...he's as close to earth as his heritage."

Pettit continued: "Everything he does is so basic. His teams block and tackle like no other teams ever to play in the Southwest Conference. He never wakes up in a dream world."

Jack Gallagher, the veteran scribe of the *Houston Post*, feels that Royal's "pleasing personality brings out the best in people."

Gallagher wrote a story once about Royal's fascination for people. "When he meets strangers and talk gets to what they are doing, he is just fascinated," Gallagher said. "Once in the lobby of the Shamrock Hilton in Houston Darrell was introduced to a ventriloquist. His eyes brightened. He asked the man how he talked without moving his lips...then he wondered how he threw his voice. Finally, the entertainer turned to somebody and said 'Is this guy just putting me on?'"

Gallagher said, "Royal is so interested in people, and he transmits this to the players. It's the same when he talks to a prospect...that fascination with other people...that enthusiasm for whatever the project might be...calling a play or talking to a ventriloquist...he's just an enthusiastic person with a bubbling personality...he says he likes to see people smile...he's a great P.R. (public relations) man."

Blackie Sherrod, executive sports editor of the *Dallas Times Herald*, said, "I'll say the same thing (former Governor) John Connolly said about him, 'I wouldn't want this man in politics. He doesn't overlook a detail.'"

Sherrod adds, "The man simply doesn't miss a thing."

Sam Blair, columnist for the *Dallas Morning News*, said of Royal, "Darrell is a generator. He has learned the importance of hard work and has the personality to put it across. Some coaches may have the basics but lack the personality to become a success. He has an unusual grasp of the game, and he has a tremendous knack of presenting it to his players."

Blair adds, "Royal and his coaches are always organized and moving toward a goal. You see so many programs come in, spurt, and bottom out. This never has happened to Darrell. Maybe it's his early childhood when he learned the value of a nickel. He's a super generator."

Dick Peebles, the columnist for the *Houston Chronicle*, says, "If Royal had gone to General Motors he would have wound up running the place..he has that type of leadership quality. He is so thorough in his preparations he leaves nothing to chance. He doesn't panic. Like he says he's gonna dance with those who brung him.

"Darrell has always basically been conservative. That's surprising because he was a quarterback (at Oklahoma), and they by nature are a more gambling type. He just rolls along like the Ford Motor Company, turning out a new model every year."

The Football Writers Association of America and their Coach of the Year—Darrell Royal.

Dave Campbell of the *Waco News-Tribune* said that Royal "has the ability to motivate...a consistent motivation...not up and down. He's real good at organization and has the great ability to adapt to his material. I always thought when they went to the flip-flop system so James Saxton could carry the ball more often was a master stroke. James was a great runner but not much of a blocker. Darrell came up with a system that put the ball in Saxton's hands plenty of times."

Campbell said, "Royal's teams play good sound, fundamental football. They certainly strive not to beat themselves.

His system lends itself to keeping errors to a minimum. They play tough defense. They get good material, but they also do something with it.

"I was with a group of writers recently and got into a big question game over what sports figures bring to mind 'class.' Somebody said Roger Staubach and another Jack Nicklaus, but Royal's name came up more than anyone. Of course a guy can have class and not be a big winner. Royal has a ton of class and is a winner."

Perhaps Galyn Wilkins of the *Fort Worth Star-Telegram* sums DKR up best: "I've been down on the sidelines in the fourth quarter, watching Royal pace up and down, licking his fingers and about walking out from under his ear phones. He's the same whether he's playing Nebraska in the Cotton Bowl, Arkansas in the Big Shootout, or Utah State in the season opener...he's the same way...after 14 years he's still able to get his stinger out for who they play. I don't care if they're playing Gumbo Tech, Darrell has that ole furnace going."

Orange Infusion

The day unfolds just like a scene out of an old Jimmy Stewart movie where the desk-bound brass is gathered around the telephone awaiting reports on a bombing mission. Assistant Athletic Director Bill Ellington shifts about nervously on the burnt orange carpet within arm's reach of the telephone. Darrell Royal, who is Stewart in this real life scenario, is out there somewhere dogfighting with hundreds of other college football coaches over the cream of the Texas schoolboy football talent. It is a rich crop, but competition is severe.

It has been seven years since the University of Texas landed the top running back in its own state. The Longhorns have made-do quite well without the No. 1 back, winning six consecutive Southwest Conference titles. But it is a stigma the Longhorns want to erase. Earl Campbell, the fabulous, fleet-foot from Tyler, John Tyler High School has promised to sign with Royal at 8 o'clock that morning.

The signing of schoolboy athletes on the second Tuesday of each February in Texas is the lifeblood of SWC schools. Over 1,000 high schools annually field football teams in Texas. Raiders swoop in from every major conference in the country, and Oklahoma is always particularly deadly. Besides the nine SWC schools—eight of which are in Texas—the state has dozens of colleges in the Lone Star, Southland Conferences, and independent ranks which nab a top player or two.

This is THE DAY for infusion of orange blood into the proud Longhorn tradition. The telephone jangles. Ellington's arm flicks out like a bull whip. His face grows red, and he slams down the phone.

"It was some guy wanting to know where he could reserve a handball court," Ellington mumbles. "Well, no news is good news," he adds bravely.

By now other Texas assistants begin calling with the names of recruits who have committed their collegiate football careers to the campus by the Colorado River. But no call from Royal. Has something gone wrong?

Sports Information Director, Jones Ramsey, gulps down a breakfast of candy corn and tells Ellington: "Keep me posted."

Bill Little, the assistant SID, can stand it no longer. He telephones the *Tyler Morning Telegraph*.

"Did we sign Campbell?" he asks. "Great, glad to hear it."

Royal has signed the 6-foot, 180-pound bluechipper and told the Tyler press, "Now let's see if we can go out and get Earl some teammates. We started our recruiting like a lot of other schools wanted."

By nightfall Royal will have left the small frame house where he signed Campbell to fly to Kilgore, Texarkana (Arkansas), Caldwell, Galveston, Houston, Abilene, Dallas, and back to Kilgore again.

"I've never seen Darrell more determined to recruit well even though he hates it," says one office orange blood.

Although Royal has won more SWC games than any other coach and owns a record in SWC titles, he is a man possessed on recruiting day, February 12, 1974. Nebraska ripped Texas 19-3 on New Year's Day and Royal says, "That's the reason my coattail has been flapping. I did not like the tonic put on me January 1..."

The telephones on the second floor of the UT athletic complex in Memorial Stadium ring constantly as writers from across the state call to chart the signing progress.

"It's bad...we've lost four guys who had committed," says a disgusted Ellington at mid-morning. "I know the coaches are mad about it."

Signees who have promised orally to come, and back off, cause a school to take some borderline players of questionable quality. It is the first times Texas has had four players change their minds in thirteen years. Under the NCAA thirty limit scholarship rule, Ellington does not see it as a particularly good omen.

But Ellington, UT's recruiting coordinator, is not gloomy long. Before he can gulp down a handful of cheese twistees and a sandwich at his desk, the sweet reports cross his desk.

Of Texas' first twenty signatures, ten of them are listed as the top prospects in the state not including swift all-State halfback Graylon Wyatt of Texarkana, Arkansas, who ignores Arkansas coach Frank Broyles' pleas to become a Razorback.

Texas defensive coach, Mike Campbell, is not so sure but adds, "That's the first thing I want to see him do when he gets here."

The day has gone well—the best recruiting twenty-four hours since the "Steve Worster Bunch" in 1967. Texas has signed the most blacks in one day in its history—six, including Campbell and Wyatt. Stories planted by some coaches that Royal is a racist have not held water.

All-American fullback Roosevelt Leaks, Lonnie Bennett, Lionell Johnson, and Raymond Clayborn have taken the blacks on tours of the campus. They have told the potential prospects that Royal is fair. Since Julius Whittier became the first Texas black letterman in 1970, more blacks have found a home at Texas.

Leak's success as the Longhorns' first star running back has cemented the feeling that if you have talent Royal will find you a position on the team. Leaks was not highly recruited out of Brenham, but Campbell had over 200 offers.

Campbell chose Texas because: "I liked what I saw, what I heard...the campus looked beautiful, and the people were friendly...they offered to help me get my education.

"Texas did not buy me. Blacks are through selling themselves...or at least I'm not going to sell myself...Texas offered me everything legal, and there was none of this stupid talk of cars and money."

Leaks is in the Longhorn office now, wearing a cut-away orange jersey and swigging on orange soda pop.

Told Campbell has signed, Leaks smiles and says, "He's The Man."

A bystander tells the story about an opposing coach's description of Campbell: "I met superman today. He wears No.

20 and plays halfback for John Tyler High School."

Leaks jokes, "Naw, he's just The Man. I'm Superman." (Weeks later after receiving the Texas Amateur Athlete of the Year award, Leaks who holds SWC season and single game rushing records suffers a damaging knee injury in spring practice and is lost for the season. Asked about his role in the recruiting, Leaks says, "I told it like it is...like you see it. You will get a chance to play at Texas. Texas has problems like all schools, but the man (Royal) is fair."

James Street, the hero of the Big Shootout against Arkansas in 1969 which earned Texas the national title, drops in. He is told Royal has flown to Tyler and signed Campbell.

"Boy, I remember when they signed me," Street says. "Ellington told me if I wasn't at the airport when they got there at 8:00 a.m. I could forget it."

"Oh, James, you always exaggerate," Ellington chides.

"OK, you really gave me to 8:15 a.m.," Street laughs.

Coaches and recruiters begin to drift into the athletic offices now to exchange battle stories of the day. They are spirited. Things look good.

Recruiter Kenneth Dabbs tells of last minute pressure put on Campbell by Oklahoma. It happened late Monday night as Dabbs sat in the Campbell home. Earl Campbell's mother is resting in bed with high blood pressure and a bad case of jitters. She believes she has a touch of the flu, but the doctor says her blood pressure is up because of worry about the recruiting of her son.

Dabbs says, "At fifteen minutes to eleven the phone rang, and it was one of the Oklahoma coaches...she kinda raised up.

"The Oklahoma coach says, 'I would like to talk to you, and Earl says, 'It's too late...I'll talk to you tomorrow at 4 o'clock.'

"The Oklahoma coach says, 'Why can't I just come on out there now?' He (Earl) says, 'Man, I've got to go to school tomorrow.'"

The Sooner recruiter tells Campbell that head coach, Barry Switzer, will be in town Thursday.

Campbell replies, "Don't send Coach Switzer down here on just a special trip for me. He probably has more important things to do."

Why autumn is something special at the University of Texas. Students examing the national championship spoils.

Dabbs says, "Mama kept raising up and kept losing her smile. Earl finally had to get indignant with them and said, 'I will talk to you at 4 o'clock tomorrow by phone' and hung up."

Campbell's mother raised up on her elbows and barked, "Earl, I'm lying here sick in bed and one of the reasons I am is my blood pressure is high and it is nerves and the main reason is because of those Oklahoma coaches."

It is a victory over hated rival Oklahoma, and the coaches love it.

In another instance Texas swoops in to take lineman Alec Beck of Austin Westlake, who switched at the last minute to "go where my heart is."

Baylor coach, Grant Teaff, makes a desperate last second telephone call with other Bear recruiters standing in the kitchen of the Beck home. Some words are exchanged. The conversation ends abruptly—another Longhorn in the bag.

At Texarkana word sifts in on how the skirmish went for Wyatt, one of the top running back prospects in Arkansas. It is a classic duel between Broyles and Royal.

Alvin Matthews, a defensive back for Green Bay who coaches at UT in the spring, is in Texarkana "baby sitting" until signing day. After midnight, while Wyatt's mother and father are out playing bingo, Matthews decides to go back to his motel room. Royal is to fly in early that morning for the signing.

Mr. and Mrs. Wyatt come home and their son cannot be found. Arkansas has apparently taken the lad for a last-minute pep talk.

As a Texas recruiter puts it, "Mama finds out where Graylon is, and it's all over for Arkansas. Essie Wyatt doesn't like it and berates Arkansas recruiter Marvin Johnson. The deal was for Alvin and Mervin to go into the room, and when the kid made his choice they were pulled off. That Friday afternoon Broyles has the office guarded, and Richard Williams has one end of the gym patrolled. Mervin has the other end of the gym guarded."

The next day Wyatt walks into Texarkana, Arkansas, High School Coach Swede Lee's office, and Matthews and Johnson are waiting. Coach Royal and Broyles have agreed by telephone that after the kid commits to one school the other will leave him alone.

A Texas insider says, "Frank thought he had a perfect deal."

Wyatt says, "Coach Johnson, I don't want to hurt anybody's feelings, but I'm going to Texas."

"You're what?" Johnson asks.

Johnson makes the drive to a nearby parking lot to tell Broyles.

"How did it go, how did it go?" Broyles asks, clapping his hands.

Johnson says "It's all over...he's going to Texas."

An unbelieving Broyles calls Lee that night for confirmation.

Coach Royal arrives the next day to sign Wyatt.

Signing days trigger hundreds of major skirmishes before a team is fielded for public viewing in the fall. No one recruiting season is like another. The scrap is a nasty one. A lot of money is spent, and a lot of names are called. Some schools cheat. There have been sixteen signing days in Royal's regime. The results have been nine SWC titles and three national crowns.

"I'm proud to say we've kept our program clean...there are no under the table deals here." Royal says.

Royal finds recruiting the most distasteful part of football.

"It's all backwards. The kids should be coming to us, not us going to them," Royal says.

In 1974 Royal has won another recruiting war. Or has he?

"I can tell you how good it was in about three years," he says.

Recruiting day will always be like that, and there will be no national championships without productive ones.

The Minority Stigma

To see Darrell Royal pitching washers with Mexican-Americans on the backstreets of Austin or vacationing with country and western singer Charley Pride or driving one hundred miles to see Johnny Rodriguez perform, you wonder how any sane person could consider him a racist. The way his luck has run on the minority question it is amazing someone has not branded him a "White Uncle Tom" because of his love for Mexican food.

It is no laughing matter to Royal. He has been stung and hurt by untruths. Some opposing coaches and recruiters unearth every tidbit they can find to keep talented blacks from the "home" locker room at Memorial Stadium.

In 1970 an article written by Bob Greene of the Associated Press' Milwaukee bureau said that Royal and four other coaches met with black coaches in Washington, D. C., on January 12, 1970. The article included the quote..."The black coach has not reached the point where his coaching is as scientific as it is in the major colleges."

It was attributed to Royal who was accepting the AP national championship trophy from Mr. Lyndon Johnson at the Longhorn football banquet. Although he felt the wire service should be punished by a libel suit for the "total lie," Royal let the matter drop after an apology was published.

Greene admitted later he had been duped by a source he considered a friend.

The story still haunts him on his recruiting travels. Royal says, "I think the success of our blacks have really have helped us in our recruitment. They now are in the position of having the attentive ear of recruits who come in and visit. The fact they can tell someone that Texas is a good place to come has counteracted the opposing schools coming in and telling the blacks how bad it is here and what a big racist Royal is and how Texas is a racist school. It's still going on right now. People are still going on right now. People are still going around digging up stories."

Royal says if he had known what he knows now he might have sued the AP because of the story out of Washington, D. C.

"If I were the age then that I am now and that many more years of coaching behind me, I would have thought much longer about following through with it because of the damage it has done," Royal says: "This has hurt me in recruiting and has hurt me with just straight friendship of blacks. It has made them very leery to be around me. They might like what they see and might like what they are experiencing when they are with me in person, but they still have it in their head that this is a devious, slick SOB we're dealing with...that we've got to watch him because he'll hurt us."

Royal says an example of how the story hurts occurred in a 1974 visit with Texas Southern coach Tom Williams, a black. Royal says: "I asked Tom if he remembered the story, and he said 'Yes, I sure do.' I said, Well, Tom, do you remember the retraction and the apology and the threatened libel suit? He said 'No.' I said, 'Do you mean in your head that story has been implanted there, and you didn't see all that publicity that followed after?' He said, 'No.' I gave him the whole story, and said this must make you feel kind of funny sitting here eating breakfast with me when this thing was in the back of your head and you didn't know it had been corrected or anything. He said, 'Well, I had thought about it. I'm glad you told me.'"

Royal says he spends the majority of his recruiting time on defense. "I'd say a good 90 percent of my time is on recruiting because a lot of the opposing recruiters put us in that posture. They use excerpts from *Meat on the Hoof*...they take excerpts from that coaching deal...

"I ran into a kid (Kilgore end) Lewis Sibley, and I knew he was bothered. I've kind of learned to get to the heart of these things. I finally got it out of him. He said he liked what he saw, but people had been telling him so much what a big racist I was.

I said let me see if I can kind of hit at some of these points.

"Have you heard that I said that blacks were not qualified to coach at all-Star games? He said 'Yes, that's one of them.' Now this goes back to five years ago...that had been hammered home to him.

"I had a black visiting with me at the time that knew the entire story...the whole thing, and so he laid that out to him."

Royal says the race issue is not the only rumor he has to combat about Texas.

"I also spend 90 percent of my time on defense that Texas is a 'big ole cold school'...that you'll just be a number and they run you through like cattle...or everybody is smoking marijuana in class...you get lost on the football team...you're kid's gonna come back with long hair, a beard and main-lining...this is the kind of thing I run into constantly."

Meat on the Hoof was written by Gary Shaw, who was a reserve guard on the 1963-67 Texas team. The book depicted Royal as a coach who treated his players like cattle and would stop at no means to win. Many former players leaped to Royal's defense.

About the same time, the book came out in 1972, the AP's Austin Bureau moved a five-part series dealing with blacks in an effort to give an accurate picture of their relationship with Royal and the school. Although the blacks interviewed never claimed they were misquoted, they said the comments did not come out the way they had intended.

Royal brought up the book and the series at the Longhorn Club in 1972 and said, "I don't know any other way to run our program except to try and be fair and honest and win, within the bounds of ethics. Any time you have somebody sitting on the bench you've got a potential family of enemies."

In *The Darrell Royal Story* by Jimmy Banks, Royal said of his reputation on race relations: "I'm just tired of trying to defend it. I'm just going to go by my record and my deeds and my thoughts and, eventually, the record is going to be tallied up. I'm going to do what I think is right and do the very best job I can and, in the end, I think it will be tallied up right. But in the meantime I guess I'm just not going to be able to convince people that I don't beat my wife and I don't kick blacks."

In 1974 prospective blacks visiting the UT campus were taken on tours by the black varsity football players.

Royal says, "All I asked them (the blacks) to do was tell it like it is...if you're good enough you'll get a chance to play...we're all treated the same...there's not any difference between black and white making the football...the University of Texas has some problems here like everybody else has, but there aren't any more problems here than there are other places.

"That's the point they (the blacks) get across to them. If you like what you see, don't worry about hidden things because there aren't any hidden things around here. But if you don't like it, don't come. But if you do like it and you're enjoying your visit...you are liking what you are seeing, then you are seeing the right thing."

The Sledgehammer

Hewn of mahogany, he looked resplendent and indestructible in a sharp tuxedo that ceremonious February night. Roosevelt Leaks, three years earlier an unsought high school player from Brenham, was in Dallas to receive the Texas Amateur Athlete of the Year award from the Texas Sportswriters Association.

He sat calmly during the cocktail hour chatting with several reporters about his remarkable 1973 season...perhaps the most astonishing in Southwest Conference history. Rawhide Rosey...or Roto Rooter Rosey, as scribe Blackie Sherrod liked to call him...had established a conference one-year rushing record of 1,415 yards.

On national television against Southern Methodist the burnt orange battering ram had done something never equaled in SWC annals. He bashed his way 342 yards against SMU defenders who dogged his every move...a University of Texas and a SWC single game record. The all-time national record is 350 yards.

"I'm more nervous right now than I've ever been on a football field," Leaks said, noting his moist palms.

But he accepted the award that night with grace and aplomb.

A month later he was on his back in a hospital, victim of torn ligaments in his knees during a 1974 spring scrimmage. Texas coach Darrell Royal had to sadly announce the loss of Leaks for the year.

Recruit an all-American like Roosevelt Leaks and watch your Wishbone-T offense purr.

"It (the Wishbone-T offense) just isn't the same without Roosevelt in there," Royal said.

Leaks was the first great black back to play under Royal.

He followed in the cleats of Steve Worster, a thundering runner who burst onto the collegiate football scene in Royal's Wishbone-T. The gifted, talented Worster, who led Texas to two national titles, was a hard act to follow.

A coach once called Royal to ask about putting in the

triple option offense, and Royal said, "What you really need is my fullback."

Whether Worster or Leaks was Texas' greatest fullback will trigger hearthside debates for decades.

Out of Bridge City, Texas, Worster broke tackles like a Brahman bull running through cane. He was tough and a winner. Somehow it was all expected from the schoolboy all-American sought by nearly every college in the land.

Leaks had anonymity and now has the Longhorn rushing records. The odds were long for a black from a country town making it big.

The only question that will be raised about Leaks was his durability—although he always scratched back when injured.

He carried fourteen consecutive times in one game before the referee found him sprawled unconscious under a pile of players. Somebody in the press box wondered: "What's wrong with Leaks?"

Dan Cook, pundit of the *San Antonio Express-News*, said, "He fainted when they didn't give him the ball."

Leaks once said, "I want to be remembered as giving 110 percent all the time...sometimes—when I'm injured—it may be only 100 percent."

Leaks, a silent type around strangers but a kidder and quipster with his friends, needed just 700 yards to break the career SWC rushing record when he was injured. He said he will pass up pro football for the 1975 season.

A teammate, Lonnie Bennett, perhaps offers the best insight into Texas' all-time ground-gaining star:

"He has a lot of inner stuff about him...he has a real deep drive to succeed. It's nothing he will talk about."

Bennett continues, "There is a quiet intensity about him. If he doesn't know what he is talking about, he won't say anything. He grew up just like most black young people I know, except that he grew up in the country and from living in the country he may have gotten help to put things into perspective. There isn't the falseness out there that there is in some cities. Roosevelt comes across straight."

And of Leaks' legend in Texas football history?

"I think he has provided an image of a black super star for us," Bennett says. "It may not help us in recruiting today, but kids are growing up now who idolize him. In five years it will make a big difference."

In February, 1974, black schoolboy super star Earl Campbell signed with Texas. Leaks may have left his name on more than the record books in Longhorn football.

DKR And Hanging Out

The wear of the recruiting war clearly showed on the man's face. Too many late nights and early wakeups do the same thing to Darrell Royal's eyes as to your's and mine. The eyes were rubbed red, and he was physically drained a full day after coaches had descended like chicken hawks on the best of Texas' high school football players. The buzzer rang, and it was faithful secretary, Blanche, with a reminder of the noon taping at a local television station.

Royal put down his diet soft drink and told his visitor, "Come on. I'm going to teach you how to hang out in Austin."

The "hanging out" was to last until 4 o'clock the next morning as DKR sought to uncoil from the unsavory mission of courting athletes for the privilege of giving them a college education to play football.

The car door had not slammed before country and western singer Charlie Rich's newest album was unreeling its honey smooth sounds.

"I enjoy it," Royal says of the music. "It says a lot...it expresses a lot of my feelings at times."

Rich is singing "A Very Special Love Song," and Royal says, "Those guys are poets...listen to the piano...hear the guitar? Do you know that Pig Robbins, the guy accompanying Charlie on the piano, is a blind black but makes over $100,000 a year in Nashville...listen...isn't that great?"

Some of Royal's closest buddies are in the recording business...Rich, Willie Nelson, Tom T. Hall, Johnny Rodriguez,

Jerry Max Layne, Charley Pride, Waylon Jennings, Kris Kristofferson...Billy Joe Shaver...Jerry Jeff Walker...Roy Clark...Alex Harvey...

"They've experienced some of the same life I have," Royal says. "But my ambitions and goals are opposed to some of my picker friends...I envy them that they can have the attitude they do...listen to the words in this song: 'Movin' is the closest thing to bein' free'..."

Royal gazes out the window while stopping at a red light and equates his position with his friends' and says somberly, "I can't move to the point where I can't take care of my responsibilities." He adds, "How does that Kristofferson song go? 'Freedom's just another word for nothing left to lose'... What they are saying is that they aren't willing to sacrifice their freedom for material things. I'm opposed with some of their lifestyles...it's not offensive...I just can't live that way."

Royal says, "You know I spend part of my time doing things I detest...now those pickers—they're GONE when something presses them...you'll get a good case of GONE trying to tie them down."

He recalls the Headliners Club Awards dinner in February, and someone asked Nelson to come to the Austin event which honors newsmen from across the state.

"Sure, I'd love to," Nelson says.

"Have you got a tux?"

"You're looking at it," replied Nelson, who was wearing blue jeans and a T-shirt.

Royal laughs at the incident.

"You know, we rented him a tux and also got some for the members of his band," Royal recalls. "It knocked him back when he saw them. They got a big kick out of it, and so did I."

Royal continues, "Now that Billy Joe Shaver, he's got two changes—a dirty one and a clean one. His movin' is no problem."

Relaxing and becoming more animated, Royal pulls into the parking lot and says, "You know I've got my frustrations, but I guess I really enjoy doing all of it. It sounds kind of contradictory doesn't it?"

"I used to come to work with my tie on all the time...I just decided one day 'These darn things are uncomfortable'...I just

Royal bending an ear to country and western star Roy Clark at the pro-am preceding the 1973 Colonial National Golf Invitational Tournament in Fort Worth.

don't wear 'em anymore."

He turns off the ignition and says, "I have touches of that (country picker's) lifestyle...in small doses...in small doses."

The studio taping takes a little longer than expected, DKR flubs a few lines and is too long-winded on another occasion. He finally gets the taping correct—to be used at the football banquet—and someone says, "Big and Beautiful, baby." Royal smiles.

It is an inside joke about a professional who spends a frustrating day trying to tape a 60-second commercial spot and ends up storming from the studio, spewing cuss words, and shouts in one sequence..."Big and Beautiful."

Royal loves inside jokes. Another relaxant.

Off to a place called appropriately "The Hideout." Royal and his visitor are the only gringos in the establishment. The others are Mexican Americans, and they gather around Royal in warm handshakes and ice cold beer.

Outside, under a tin roof, there's a "washer pit." Royal twirls the washers with a special spin that causes the metal to bite like a soft wedge shot on the rubber mat surrounding a hole barely the size of the washer. Royal's opponent caroms a washer off the concrete wall behind the mat, and laughter explodes.

"Amigo, you hold it this way" a bystander demonstrates and hangs a washer over the edge of the hole. Ooohs and Ahhhs.

"That's pretty good" Royal says, "but the champion around here is 72-years old, and he makes one out of every four...let's eat."

The food—calf liver, frijoles, and ground meat wrapped in a tortilla—is washed down with beer at the jukebox. Rodriguez is singing "Riding My Thumb to Mexico."

"I talked 'em into putting Johnny on the box...everything else is in Spanish," Royal says between bites. A pleasant, brown-skinned young man approaches the table, introduces himself, and inquires if Royal has had any luck recruiting a Chicano.

"Not yet; as you know Cesar Moreno transferred and Rene Amaya graduated so we'd like to find somebody,...and we will."

"I know you will keep trying...thanks Mr. Royal," the man says pleasantly and leaves.

A friend of Royal's drops by the table and mentions that Rodriguez is playing San Antonio at the livestock show. Royal's eyes sparkle like a shiny plateglass window.

In minutes Royal has been on the telephone and arranged for a quick trip to San Antonio. Within hours he is on the road with a friend and wife, Edith.

"You can't get it any sweeter than this," he proclaims.

Royal worries on the trip whether he has gotten the correct instructions to the livestock coliseum.

"Oh, Darrell," Edith kids, "you could get lost a block from your home."

He follows a horse trailer right on target to the coliseum.

"See, Edith, see," he says, knowingly, as Edith Royal, a trim handsome woman, rolls her eyes heavenward.

In a matter of hours Royal has been transformed from a man on the verge of being an ulcer candidate to a 48-year-old kid in a malt shop. Rodriguez is wheeling into his first number as the Royal party finds its seats. He is singing "That's the Way Love Goes..." and the jammed crowd is high volt electricity.

"Man, he got some kind of stage presence since I saw him last...uh, huh," Royal says.

Rodriguez makes a special introduction of Royal, and the crowd politely applaudes. A half-hour later Rodriguez throws his sequined jacket into the crowd, and a grandmother gets into a tug-o-war with two teenagers. Granny loses and gets only a handful of sequins for her trouble. Royal laughs. On the way to the Gunter Hotel after the performance, Royal tells about the first time he met Rodriguez.

"He was playing in Tom T's band for $25.00 a night," Royal says. "He had hitchhiked to Nashville with $5.00 in his pocket to get the job. Hall recognized his talent and booted him out saying 'Son, you've got so much going you don't need me.'"

Royal relishes the story. During the depression he hitchhiked from California to Oklahoma with a ball and glove in an old Victrola box just to play for Hollis High School and start his career. What the men have in common is obvious.

The Rodriguez suite is a mob scene, not what Darrell had hoped.

"We might get down to some serious pickin' if all these folks clear out," he says.

That is the way Royal relaxes best, with his shoes off, sitting on a rug, propped up against the wall with something cold, listening to his picker friends.

He only asks one thing: If you cannot be quiet, please leave so the soul soothing sounds get the proper reception.

No "shoe kickin'" session is in the cards this night because of the crowd, and the DKR trio finds his car and wheels in the direction of Austin.

On the road back, "Dan Cook's Time-Out" hoves into view. It's 1:30 a.m., but Royal is still going strong.

Cook is a sportswriter for the *San Antonio Express News* and a friend of Royal's.

"I've been wanting to see Dan's place, even if he doesn't understand that pickin' music," Royal says.

The visit is pleasant with Cook reopening his delicatessen as everyone swaps stories. Before he leaves, Royal signs a picture of himself on the rest-room door.

"That's better than being nowhere at all," he bellows.

It is 4:00 a.m. when Royal's car touches his driveway. The Willie Nelson tape is going strong. Darrell Royal is home and relaxed—ready to resume his pressure-cooker role as athletic director and head football coach at the largest university in Texas. That is the way Darrell Royal really is. That is the way Darrell Royal always will be.

Home Sweet Home

The fact that Darrell Royal has never heeded the call to return to his alma mater at Oklahoma or entered the ranks of professional coaching remains a mystery to many. But these people do not know him well. He feels comfortable at the University of Texas where he does not have to come to work in a tie and can hop over to "The Backdoor" or "El Ranchos" for a quick dose of Mexican food and a beer.

He has more power and prestige than he really cares for and enough money to live without strain. He may gag on the unsavoriness of high school recruiting but can clear the air with just one "pickin' session" with his friends from the country and western music world.

As recently as January, 1974, Royal was mentioned in connection with the head coaching job of the New York Giants of the National Football League.

Royal says, "I'm not one to toy with happiness...it's very hard to come by. I am happy in my coaching position here...everybody has problems, but I can't think of a place I would be happier. There are only two reasons why I see a guy in my position would want to leave and coach professional football."

He says to coach pro ball is "a little more glamorous...a little more celeb type...more broadway and flashing light type job than I have. Well, I'm just as big as I want to be.

"The other thing would be more money," Royal says. "I don't have a lot of money, but I have enough that I'm

Royal and former Oklahoma Coach Chuck Fairbanks exchange observations after another Red River showdown between the two rivals.

Coach Royal and a 1966 chat with all-Southwest Conference Diron Talbert and kicking specialist David Conway. Not many players wear cowboy hats on campus anymore.

Darrell Royal in a lonely moment of decision on the sidelines.

comfortable, and people have been so nice to me—and I mean Texas alumni—that I've lived in many instances like I have money. And what difference does it make?"

He adds, "I would be deathly afraid to take another assignment just for money and get up there and find out I'm unhappy. I could go take that money and lay it out on the bed and look at it every night and it wouldn't make me happy. Damn, if I was miserable, I would know I was miserable."

Royal says he is near his children and his grandchildren in Austin.

"I've got too big an investment...I've been coaching seventeen years at the University of Texas," Royal says. "I've traveled the state over those years, and it's a huge investment in time. This ring I wear is a ring I give every graduating senior. I buy them personally, and now doctors and lawyers scattered all over the state wear them. This means something to me that's hard to explain. This type of friendship and bond makes college coaching very rewarding. At my age I'd hate to pick up and start over."

After Royal was rumored for the Giant job in early 1974 he said, "I've analyzed the situation and decided that I'm so far in debt that I'll never get out of it, and I might as well be in debt where it's warm."

Of course Royal said the "debt" part with tongue-in-cheek, but the story spread across the country. About a week later he was making an airline reservation and overheard the reservationist telling someone: "It's poor Darrell Royal on the telephone. You've heard he's broke, haven't you?"

Edith Royal later heard Darrell's quote on television and asked, "Did you say that?"

"Yeh, I said that."

"Well, do you think that's right to mislead people?"

Darrell replied, "Mislead them about what?"

"About being so far in debt," Edith followed.

"Heck, Edith, you don't see any humor in it?" Royal said.

Edith replied, "Well, I do, but I don't think a lot of people will see it humorously."

No matter whether people get his one-liners, DKR plans on keeping his roots in Austin where he can live like he has money.

World's Tallest Fat Man

To draw a maximum crowd, a circus barker would bill him as the (self-proclaimed) "World's Tallest Fat Man." It would not be nearly as exciting to call him simply the finest sports information director in America. The only crowd the barker could draw would be sportswriters looking for a can of beer, two or three hundred jokes, and the latest update on the University of Texas football team.

Writers love the six-foot-four, ???? pounds Jones Ramsey because they can count on him to sweat blood and perhaps a droplet or two of jalapeno sauce to provide the finest working conditions in any press box in the Southwest. Ramsey has personally wrestled free-loaders out of the press box. His stats are the fastest in the west, and Ramsey has even gone so far as to have the best Mexican food this side of Tampico (El Ranchos) catered to the hungry hordes. You guard your meal ticket like it was an 1893 ten-dollar gold piece. His talents provide an immeasurable service to the University of Texas—providing information and keeping sometimes surly writers in a good mood at the same time.

"Texas writers have made honest people out of us," says Ramsey, who was the 1974 president of the College Sports Information Directors of America. "We're not publicity men or flacks. No longer does a publicity man's job depend on writing somebody's column. My first obligation to the press is to make sure the free-loaders are not in the way. Writers are on deadlines, and it makes me mad when somebody keeps me from taking care of them. It's like Jack Gallagher told me one time, 'You don't have to do a thing for me but give me a seat when I come to work and see that I'm left alone.'"

Ramsey does it with a flamboyancy all his own, starting pregame night at the press headquarters, 2001 Villa Capri. Many a writer without a reservation has spent the night there in various states of dress on the couch, on the rug, or propped up in a chair.

"How you hittin' 'em?" is Ramsey's greeting at the door as he drums a forefinger on a glass of Scotch and pops a beer in your hand.

What Ramsey is asking is "How's life? How you doin'?"

He is not asking your golf score.

Ramsey is a speechmaker, goodwill ambassador, and Darrell Royal's left hand. He just might be the quickest quip in the world.

"I'm sick and tired of waking up every morning sick and tired," Ramsey bellows after a night of partying. I nicked my neck shaving this morning and I'm glad...it gave my eyeballs a chance to drain."

Ramsey, a native of Oklahoma who cut his teeth in the newspaper business at the *Stillwater Daily News* prior to coming to the Southwest Conference, says, "I love being around writers, good writers. I love being around winners, and that's what we've got here in the state of Texas...there are more good writers here than in any other part of the country."

One of Ramsey's finest jobs came when Texas was renovating Memorial Stadium. The writers were huddled in a wooden and wire coop called affectionately the "chicken–coop."

"We held Shootout II with Arkansas in there and it was jammed, but we didn't get one single complaint," Ramsey recalls with pride.

Ramsey has a sense of humor as large as his appetite for nachos. During the week preceding the Great Shootout I in 1969, writers converged on Austin in droves to quiz the Longhorns about the showdown in Arkansas. Blackie Sherrod was one of the first to arrive only to be met at the airport by Ramsey who had a grim look on his face.

"Sorry, Blackie, there won't be any interviews of James Street," Ramsey said in stern tones. "He's afraid he'll hurt his concentration if he talks to the press."

Sherrod's crisp brown Comanche features turned scarlet. "I might as well catch a plane right back out of here," Sherrod growled.

"Come on, and you might see some of the players at the dining hall," Ramsey pleaded.

Sherrod walked to a waiting car, handed his luggage to a young porter, hopped in the back seat, and slammed the door. He looked up to see the smiling driver: James Street.

"You should have seen Blackie's face," Ramsey recalls with relish.

Mickey Herskowitz of the *Houston Post* says it is amazing how "ten or twelve years later Jones can quote back to you the lead you wrote on a certain game most people have long forgotten."

Ramsey followed capable Bill Sansing and Wilbur Evans as the SID at the University of Texas. Ramsey came from Texas A&M where he had such a fondness for his boss Paul "Bear" Bryant that he named a son after him. Bryant later moved to Alabama, and Jim Myers, who was somewhat sensitive to the Bryant legacy, was the replacement.

Herskowitz recalls that "Freshmen were quitting under Myers at a rapid rate, and Myers got to the point where he told Ramsey to soft-pedal it. Now Myers had to go out of town and turned his local television show over to Ramsey, who had old friend, trainer Smokey Harper, as an easy guest.

"Harper was a legendary trainer of a breed long disappeared. He was another leftover from the Bryant regime. Jones and Harper chatted on the show for a while, and finally Jones said, 'Now, Smokey, tell us about those great Aggie freshmen.'

"'Well, Jones, we got some good folks if the coaches don't run 'em off,'" Smokey shot back.

"Ramsey gulped and turned to the camera: 'And now folks, a word from Lily Ice Cream.'"

Some of Ramsey's one-liners have gotten him into hot water with Royal. Probably the worst, as far as Ramsey was concerned, occurred in 1971 in Los Angeles. Someone asked Jones at the NCAA basketball tournament about the Longhorn thump-thump program.

"There are only two sports at Texas...football and spring

Jones Ramsey and son, Paul, at famed 2001, headquarters for media covering University of Texas football. As Ramsey signifies, he's No. 1 in the business like the Longhorn football teams.

football," Ramsey cackled.

Ramsey said, "It's one of the worst things that ever happened to me. You know, I just spout those things out like ole faithful. Well, it went all over the country and got back to

Darrell, and he chewed my tail out and rightfully so. We have an all-around program at Texas, and we're proud of it."

He said although the storied Arkansas-Texas game in 1969 received the most national attention, the biggest demand for tickets was the 1963 Baylor-Texas collision in Memorial Stadium. Texas' 1963 national champions edged Baylor 7-0 when Duke Carlisle, rushed into the defensive secondary by Royal, intercepted a Don Trull pass in the dying moments. Not only was Ramsey trying to keep the press box functioning but he had to give a play-by-play over the telephone of what was happening, to a big Longhorn supporter who had called from San Francisco.

"I almost had a heart attack," Ramsey said. "That was the biggest one (game) I've had."

Everyone has his own particular Ramsey story.

One particular favorite is the year 23 Longhorns came down with the 24-hour virus. Ramsey was bombarded with telephone calls but deadpanned, "The worst trouble was learning to spell diarrhea."

Ramsey's humorous approach prompted one writer to lead his game story, saying, "Texas ran like there was an outhouse in the end zone." The 'Horns prevailed 56-14 over the Bears that day.

Bill Morgan, publicity director of the Southwest Conference, recalls leaving the stadium with Ramsey one night when a car pulled over and the driver asked the final score.

"21-0," Ramsey said.

"Who won?" the driver asked.

"The 21," Ramsey replied.

Ramsey is a dedicated man who says, "I enjoy going to work in the morning. Isn't it great to be able to say that? So few people can."

He spends quiet weekends at the lake with his good friend Bill Molitare, an Austin architect, and their families.

There is space for only one more Ramsey story, and it is my favorite because in it he is the victim of his own security system to keep "hangers-on" out of the press box.

Ramsey wheeled into the parking lot at Memorial Stadium two years ago, but did not have the proper identification card. He had everything else—a UT system automobile, a Texas

Relays hat, a billfold full of identification cards, everything but the proper pass.

Ramsey was livid, and he pointed to the press box shouting at the gatekeeper: "I make my living up there...I've got a track meet to run...don't you know who I am?"

"Oh, I know you're Jones Ramsey, but you told me nobody—and that means nobody—gets through here without the right pass. You'll have to get yours," the attendant replied.

Jones Ramsey can appreciate a man doing his job. Texas football is more famous because Ramsey has done his so well.

Royalisms

Darrell Royal is a sportswriter's delight with his colorful phrases known as "Royalisms." For example he was asked before the 1974 Cotton Bowl game with Nebraska whether he was bored by his sixth consecutive trip to the New Year's Day Classic. Royal grinned and answered, "I'd like to borrow a saying from one of my picker friends. 'Too much ain't enough and like as not will never be.'" It was vintage Royal. Instead of just answering "no" Royal gave the scribes something they could hang a lead on. It was the top story in a lot of newspapers the next day. For posterity here are some of the best of the "Royalisms."

"We're gonna dance with the ones who brung us."

"Ole ugly is better than ole nuthin.'"

"He's so rich he could burn a wet elephant."

"They're hotter than a burning stump."

"(on fancy, striped uniforms) Hell, no. I'm not going to candy this thing up. These are work clothes."

"We live one day at a time and scratch where it itches."

"You're what-iffing now and everybody can what-if."

"Punt returns will kill you before a minnow can swim a dipper."

"Every coach likes those players who, like trained pigs, will grin and jump right in the slot."

"They didn't exactly come to town on a load of wood."

"When that adrenalin starts flowing, you just get there faster than normal. You can jump higher and dive deep and

Did the lady on the billboard overhear a Royalism? How about "Ole ugly is better than ole nuthin'?"

come up dryer."

"Winning coaches must treat mistakes like copperheads in the bedclothes—avoid them with all the energy you can muster."

"Breaks balance out. The sun don't shine on the same ole dog's rear end every day."

"A little bit of perfume won't hurt if you don't drink it."

"To say we were the only ones aggressive would be like a skunk telling an opossum that his breath smells."

"One does not take over a squad that has won only one of ten games and inherit a warm bed."

"He is the kind of player who knows where his hat belongs and does a good job of putting it right between that fellow's eight and four (the opposing player wearing jersey No. 84)."

"There is no such thing as defeat except when it comes from within. As long as a person doesn't admit he is defeated, he is not defeated—he's just a little behind and isn't through fighting."

"The only thing that disturbs me about my profession is the fact that people give you too much credit when you win and too much criticism when you lose. I'll be the same person and do the same things and say the same things when we lose. But people won't believe me then. I won't change—but the people will."

"I'm the world's biggest coward. I run scared all the time. I agree with Eisenhower—just before the election, the opposition always looks twelve-feet tall."

(Royal has been called the Barry Goldwater of college football.) It is said he's so conservative he looks both ways before crossing a one-way street, to which Darrell says: "What's so crazy about that?"

(After losing a close game in the final minutes after he had taken a lead) "It was like having a big ole lollipop in your mouth and the first thing you know all you have left is the stick."

"The margin between victory and defeat is so small that you can't get too chesty when you win or too despondent when you lose. I've always been too busy with tomorrow to look back at yesterday."

After the Shootout No. 2 Arkansas game in 1970 won by

Texas 41-7, Darrell in leaving the bench to run to the dressing room said: "I couldn't even enjoy the win en route to the dressing room because I was worrying about how mad Arkansas would be next year."

"They're gonna come after us with their eyes pulled up like BBs."

"Luck is what happens when preparation meets opportunity."

At half time of the 1968 Oklahoma game when OU led 7-0: "There's a heckuva fight going on out there in the Cotton Bowl. Why don't you get in on it." Longhorns won it 9-7.

(After the game) "You ought to be wondering how you are going to calm them down to tie their shoes, but I thought I'd have to light pine knots to get them out of the dressing room before the game."

"Next to bad weather, there is no equalizer like two fired-up football teams."

"You can't invent a feeling."

"Above all, people like a winner."

"The way we look at it is that we stumped our toe at Rice and got out with a tie. How lucky can you be?"

(Asked to comment on big game coming up): "I don't feel very clever these days."

Pointing out eighteen-year-old sophomore on team: "His mother probably still tells him what time to get in."

"We're not exactly a rolling ball of butcher knives."

Commenting on story which listed Longhorn player as weighing 242: "He couldn't see if he weighed 242."

On poor coverage of kick: "You'd have thought we would be on it (the ball) like a hen on a june bug."

(A player hobbling with injury): "He's grasshopping it around."

(On rating a close game as even): "It's a hoss and a hoss."

(On losing a game in upset): "Those folks aren't exactly poverty-stricken where football players are concerned."

(Bragging about opposing passer): "He can Andy Gump it (throw an accurate short pass) or he can hum it (hit the long ones too)."

Asked why certain star back was not playing safety on punt returns: "He can't even catch his breath. We don't even let

him field them in practice without his headgear on."

"Lady Luck was on our side and we welcomed her in."

"I'd like to be considered better than the old average whacker when I set my bucket down."

"Anyone in athletics is a little bit of a ham...it all starts from the time you get your first letter...and it carries into coaching."

"Everything starts with winning...I don't see how a competitor can enjoy the parties and things if he gets beat."

On his theory that most football games are decided with a few big plays: "Football is really just like Russian roulette. Most of the time the firing pin hits an empty chamber, but you never know when the big bang is coming."

Defense has always been a byword at Texas. First Joel Brame uncorks a vicious tackle and then Jay Arnold blocks a field goal

Appendix

LONGHORN LORE

The University of Texas mascot is a Texas Longhorn steer—Bevo IX—whose colors are orange and white. Bevo VIII was retired as too unruly after docile old Bevo VII was forced into retirement by an arthritic condition in 1965 after serving as mascot for eight years.

UT's Bevos date from 1916, when Bevo I made his appearance during the Texas A&M-Texas game at Austin. That first mascot, much the same as some of his successors, had a short career. Bevo I was branded by some Aggies and later (1921) was served as steak at an A&M-Texas get-together.

The Bevos disappeared for a while after that.

Bevo II served a one-year hitch in 1936. But he was a Hereford anyhow.

Bevo III, who actually was a blue ribbon stock show winner, also served for only one year (1945).

Bevo IV, one of the stampeding kind, lasted as mascot from 1949 to 1951, when his temper caused his dismissal.

Bevo V, bought as a calf in 1951, served as mascot through 1954.

Bevo VI, about as ill-tempered as any of the mascots, nevertheless snorted through three full years (1954-57), before giving away to the "longest tenure" of them all, Bevo VII.

Then came the appearance by Bevo VIII—and now the newest in the herd, Bevo IX. He was born in February, 1966, at the Albany State Park and comes from the stock line that has furnished most of the previous Bevos.

The mascots are sponsored by the Silver Spurs, a men's honorary organization. They are loaned to the university by the state of Texas with the understanding that they will be retired after a reasonable period of time.

TEXAS FIGHT SONG

During Texas football games, when the Longhorns score, when they are on a drive, or when things may be going wrong, fans rally to the notes of the "Texas Fight" song played by the Longhorn band. Originally titled "Texas Taps," the tune has become the school's official fight song and is commonly called "Texas Fight" due to the first words of the chorus. The original melody was written in 1923 by Walter S. Hunnicut who collaborated with James E. King on the Longhorn Band arrangement. Lyrics were composed by Burnett Pharr.

"SMOKEY" THE CANNON

Though banned in recent years at Southwest Conference games, a highlight of non-conference contests is the thunderous roar of "Smokey," a cannon which fires after each Texas score. Operated by the Cowboys, a service organization, the cannon has become another well-known Longhorn tradition.

ALMA MATER—"THE EYES OF TEXAS"

"The Eyes of Texas" was written in 1903 by John Lang Sinclair, who wrote it for a minstrel show as a satire on Dr. Lambdin Prather, then president of the university. Dr. Prather had attended Washington and Lee, it was said, and when he addressed the student body always mentioned "the eyes of the South are upon you." Dr. Prather often quoted it, confining it only to Texas. There was a standing joke among the students about Dr. Prather's "all-seeing eyes." At the minstrel the song (written to the tune of "I've Been Workin' on the Railroad") became a tremendous hit and was sung far into the night. Gradually it became the school song and the unofficial song of the state.

O.U. TROPHY — BRONZE HAT

Emblematic of victory in the annual Texas-Oklahoma football game, the Bronze Hat was donated to the two schools by the State Fair of Texas in 1941. An exact replica of the famed "ten-gallon" cowboy hat, the trophy is retained by the winning school each year. The trophy includes small bronze football-shaped plaques around the edges, bearing the year and the score of the annual intersectional clash.

To the national champion goes the spoils. What recruiting day is all about.

NICKNAME – LONGHORNS

Mr. D. A. Frank (1903-1905) is the source of how the University of Texas teams became known as "Longhorns." He related in a 1943 letter to "The Firing Line" column of the *Daily Texas* that Alex Weisburg in 1903 was editor-in-chief of the *Texas* and one day told Mr. Frank, "D. A., hereafter in every sports article call the team 'The Longhorns,' and we'll soon have it named." These instructions were followed and passed down for several years, according to Mr. Frank, and "along about 1906 or 1907, the name became official..."

VICTORY SIGNAL – THE TOWER

Traditionally the Main Building ("The Tower") at the University of Texas is bathed in orange lights following a football victory or other outstanding athletic achievement (SWC and NCAA championships, national playoff victories, etc.), as well as special university occasions and holidays.

The entire building is lighted orange for Thanksgiving Day football victories only; the Tower shaft is white and the Tower orange for the achievements noted in the preceding paragraph, and the Tower shaft is white and the Tower alternately orange and white on nights of tie football games or ties for SWC championships.

Standing twenty-seven stories tall, the Tower serves as a beacon of UT's athletic success in Austin and for many miles in every direction.

TEXAS' SCHOOL COLORS

The colors Orange and White were officially adopted on May 10, 1900, after a three-cornered fight between students at the Main University, the School of Medicine, and ex-students. The colors were first used in the spring of 1884 when a special train of students went to Georgetown for a baseball game with Southwestern.

BIGGEST DRUM – "BIG BERTHA"

The world's largest bass drum, "Big Bertha," is a standout attraction whenever the Longhorn Band is in evidence. Presented to the band in 1955 by Colonel D. Harold Byrd of Dallas, Big Bertha is eight feet in diameter, fifty-four inches in width, and weighs 500 pounds. Four bandsmen, known as "Drum Wranglers," take care of the monster.

HOOK 'EM HORNS

Hook 'em Horns, the University of Texas' battle cry, originated at a pep rally before the 1955 Texas-TCU football game. The Hook 'em Horns sign is formed by extending the index and little fingers while folding the middle and ring fingers beneath the thumb. The sign represents a Longhorn steer's head.

FINE OPENING-GAMES RECORD

Texas has lost but eight openers in 80 seasons plus three other opening-game ties. First blemish was a scoreless tie with A&M in 1907. First losing opener was in 1938 when Kansas edged UT, 19-18. First opening loss in Austin was the 1955 defeat at the hands of Texas Tech by the score of 20-14. Texas has lost or tied these opening games: 1907–0-0 with Texas A&M; 1936–6-6 with LSU; 1938–18-19 to Kansas; 1953–7-20 to LSU; 1955–14-20 to Texas Tech; 1956–20-44 to Southern California; 1960–13-14 to Nebraska; 1966–6-10 to Southern California; 1967–13-17 to Southern California; 1968–20-20 with Houston; and 1973–15-20 to Miami.

MILESTONES

The Longhorns reached several new milestones during their national championship season of 1969. The Cotton Bowl win over Notre Dame was the school's 500th victory while that 15-14 victory over Arkansas at Fayetteville was UT's 200th Southwest Conference victory. Coach Darrell Royal recorded his 100th victory at Texas in the third game (Navy) in 1969.

1918 TEAM 'HOMERS'

The 1918 Texas team set something of a record. It played eight of its nine games at Austin. The only road trip resulted in a 14-0 victory over Rice at Houston.

DANA X. BIBLE COLLEGIATE COACHING RECORD

In his 33 years with college squads Dana X. Bible won 14 conference championships. His college teams won 209 games, lost 74, and tied 19.

Bible's coaching career began at Brandon Prep in his native Tennessee shortly after he graduated in 1912 from Carson-Newman College where he lettered in football, basketball, and baseball. In 1913 he moved to Mississippi College for a three-year span, taking over in October, 1916, at Louisiana State University to finish the season there. From 1917 through 1928, with 1918 off to serve as an air corps lieutenant, he coached at Texas A&M College.

The 1929 season was the first of eight successful years at Nebraska, and in 1937 he arrived at the University of Texas. His first two seasons at Texas—1937 and 1938—are the only losing years on his long record which, in won-and-lost columns, looks like this:

	No. Years	Won	Lost	Tied
Mississippi College	3	18	8	1
Louisiana State University	1	5	0	1
Texas A&M College	11	73	20	7
University of Nebraska	8	50	15	7
University of Texas	10	63	31	3
TOTAL	33	209	74	19

Notable in his victory string are these items: (1) Untied unscored-on teams at Texas A&M in 1917 and 1919 (and through 1920 till Texas won, 7-3, in the annual Thanksgiving game); (2) five Southwest Conference titles in eleven years at Texas A&M; (3) six winners in the Big Six in eight years at Nebraska; and (4) three Conference titles in his last five years at Texas.

DARRELL ROYAL'S HEAD-COACHING RECORD

At Texas:

	Conference				Full Season: (Includes Bowl Games)			
Year	Won	Lost	Tied	Pct.	Won	Lost	Tied	Pct.
1957	4	1	1	.750	6	4	1	.591
1958	3	3	0	.500	7	3	0	.700
1959	5	1	0	.833	9	2	0	.818
1960	5	2	0	.714	7	3	1	.682
1961	6	1	0	.857	10	1	0	.909
1962	6	0	1	.929	9	1	1	.864
1963	7	0	0	1.000	11	0	0	1.000
1964	6	1	0	.857	10	1	0	.909
1965	3	4	0	.429	6	4	0	.600
1966	5	2	0	.714	7	4	0	.636
1967	4	3	0	.571	6	4	0	.600
1968	6	1	0	.857	9	1	1	.864
1969	7	0	0	1.000	11	0	0	1.000
1970	7	0	0	1.000	10	1	0	.909
1971	6	1	0	.857	8	3	0	.727
1972	7	0	0	1.000	10	1	0	.909
1973	7	0	0	1.000	8	3	0	.727
TOTALS	94	20	2	.819	144	36	4	.794
1954-55-56 at Miss. State and Washington					17	13	0	.566
Career Head Coach Record (21 Years)					161	49	4	.762

TEXAS' ALL-S.W.C. PLAYERS

(This is not a complete list of Longhorns gaining all-conference recognition but a list of those achieving consensus acclaim.)

Year	Players	Year	Players
1915	Clyde Littlefield, back Pig Dittmar, center	1939	Jack Crain, back
1916	Alva Carlton, guard Pig Dittmar, center Maxey Hart, end Rip Lang, back	1940	Pete Layden, back
		1941	Malcolm Kutner, end Chal Daniel, guard Jack Crain, back Pete Layden, back
1917	Dewey Bradford, guard		
1919	Bibb Falk, tackle	1942	Stan Mauldin, tackle Roy Dale McKay, back Jackie Field, back
1920	Hook McCullough, end Swede Swenson, center Tom Dennis, tackle Grady Watson, back	1943	Joe Parker, end Franklin Butler, guard J. R. Calahan, back Ralph Ellsworth, back Joe Magliolo, back
1921	Hook McCullough, end Tom Dennis, tackle Swede Swenson, center Bud McCallum, back	1944	Hub Bectol, end Jack Sachse, center Bobby Layne, back Harold Fischer, guard
1922	Swede Swenson, center Joe Ward, tackle Ivan Robertson, back	1945	Hub Bectol, end Dick Harris, center Bobby Layne, back
1923	Oscar Eckhardt, back Ed Bluestein, tackle F. M. Bralley, center Jim Marley, back	1946	Hub Bectol, end Dick Harris, center Bobby Layne, back
1924	Bud Sprague, tackle K. L. Berry, guard	1947	Bobby Layne, back Max Baumgardner, end Dick Harris, tackle
1925	H. C. Pfannkuche, center Matt Newell, end Mack Saxon, back	1948	George Petrovich, tackle Dick Harris, center Ray Borneman, back
1926	Mack Saxon, back	1949	Bud McFadin, guard Danny Wolfe, guard
1927	Pottie McCullough, center Ike Sewell, guard	1950	Ben Procter, end Ken Jackson, tackle Bud McFadin, guard Byron Townsend, back Bobby Dillon, defensive back Don Menasco, linebacker
1928	Bill Ford, end Gordy Brown, tackle Dexter Shelley, back		
1929	Alfred Rose, end		
1930	Ox Blanton, tackle Ox Emerson, guard Lester Peterson, end Harrison Stafford, back Dexter Shelley, back Ernie Koy, back	1951	Harley Sewell, guard Tom Stolhandske, end Gib Dawson, back June Davis, linebacker Bobby Dillon, defensive back
1931	Harrison Stafford, back Ernie Koy, back	1952	Harley Sewell, guard Tom Stolhandske, end Gib Dawson, back Dick Ochoa, back T. Jones, back Billy Quinn, back Phil Branch, guard Bill Georges, defensive end
1932	Bohn Hilliard, back Harrison Stafford, back Ernie Koy, back		
1933	Bill Smith, center Bohn Hilliard, back Charley Coates, tackle	1953	Phil Branch, guard Carlton Massey, end Gilmer Spring, end
1934	Phil Sanger, end Bohn Hilliard, back Charley Coates, center	1954	Buck Lansford, tackle
1936	Hugh Wolfe, back	1955	Herb Gray, guard Walter Fondren, back Menan Schriewer, end
1937	Hugh Wolfe, back		
1938	Jack Rhodes, guard	1959	Maurice Doke, guard

	Jack Collins, halfback		Glen Halsell, linebacker
	Monte Lee, end		Bill Atessis, end
	Rene Ramirez, halfback		Tom Campbell, halfback
1960	James Saxton, back		Bob McKay, tackle
	Monte Lee, guard		Charles Speyrer, end
			Steve Worster, fullback
1961	James Saxton, back		Bobby Wuensch, tackle
	Mike Cotten, back	1970	Steve Worster, fullback
	Don Talbert, tackle		Bobby Wuensch, tackle
	Bob Moses, end		Bill Atessis, end
	David Kristynik, center		Bobby Mitchell, guard
			Scott Henderson, linebacker
1962	Johnny Treadwell, guard		Jim Bertelsen, halfback
	Tommy Ford, back		Bill Zapalac, linebacker
	Scott Appleton, tackle		Jerry Sisemore, tackle
			Mike Dean, guard
1963	Scott Appleton, tackle		Stan Mauldin, linebacker
	Tommy Ford, back		Ray Dowdy, tackle
	Tommy Nobis, guard	1971	Jerry Sisemore, tackle
1964	Tommy Nobis, guard		Jim Bertelsen, halfback
	Clayton Lacy, tackle		Ray Dowdy, tackle
	Olen Underwood, center		Greg Ploetz, tackle
	Knox Nunnally, end		Randy Braband, linebacker
	Pete Lammons, end		Donnie Wigginton, QB
	Dan Mauldin, end		Don Crosslin, guard
	Harold Philipp, back		Tommy Woodard, linebacker
	Joe Dixon, back		Alan Lowry, defensive back
1965	Tommy Nobis, guard	1972	Alan Lowry, quaterback
	Frank Bedrick, guard		Jerry Sisemore, tackle
	Pete Lammons, end		Roosevelt Leaks, back
	Diron Talbert, tackle		Bill Wyman, center
	Jack Howe, center		Travis Roach, guard
1966	Chris Gilbert, back		Randy Braband, linebacker
	Corby Robertson, end		Glen Gaspard, linebacker
	Joel Brame, linebacker		Mike Rowen, back
			Malcolm Minnick, end
1967	Chris Gilbert, back	1973	Bill Wyman, center
	Loyd Wainscott, tackle		Roosevelt Leaks, back
	Danny Abbott, guard		Malcolm Minnick, end
			Jay Arnold, back
1968	Chris Gilbert, back		Doug English, tackle
	Deryl Comer, end		Bob Simmons, tackle
	Danny Abbott, guard		Don Crosslin, guard
	Steve Worster, back		Bruce Hebert, guard
	Loyd Wainscott, tackle		Glen Gaspard, linebacker
	Glen Halsell, linebacker		Bill Rutherford, end
	Leo Brooks, tackle		Wade Johnston, linebacker
1969	Leo Brooks, tackle		

LONGHORNS' HONORED PLAYERS

ALL-AMERICA SELECTIONS

1941—Malcolm Kutner, end
1941—Chal Daniel, guard
1943—Joe Parker, end
1944-45-46—Hub Bechtol, end
1947—Bobby Layne, back
1947—Dick Harris, tackle
1949—Randall Clay, back
1949-50—Bud McFadin, guard
1950—Don Menasco, end
1951—Bobby Dillon, back
1952—Harley Sewell, guard
1952—Tom Stolhandske, end
1953—Carlton Massey, end
1955—Herb Gray, guard
1959—Maurice Doke, guard
1961—James Saxton, back
1961—Don Talbert, tackle
1962—Johnny Treadwell, guard
1963—Scott Appleton, tackle
1963—Tommy Ford, back
1964-65—Tommy Nobis, guard
1967—Corby Robertson, back
1968—Chris Gilbert, back
1968—Loyd Wainscott, tackle
1969—Bob McKay, tackle
1969-70—Bobby Wuensch, tackle
1969-70—Steve Worster, back
1969-70—Charles Speyrer, end
1970—Bill Atessis, end
1971-72—Jerry Sisemore, tackle
1973—Bill Wyman, center
1973—Roosevelt Leaks, back

EAST-WEST GAME SELECTIONS

1930—Gordy Brown, tackle
1931—Dexter Shelley, back
1933—Ernie Koy and Harrison Stafford, backs
1935—Bohn Hilliard, back
1938—Hugh Wolfe, back
1939—Jack Rhodes, guard
1940—Park Myers, tackle
1942—Chal Daniel, guard and Malcolm Kutner, end
1945—Harold Fischer, guard; Jack Sachse, center; Walter Heap, back
1946—Buddy Jungmichel, guard
1947—Spot Collins, guard; Hub Bechtol, end; Walter Heap, back
1953—Carton Massey, end; Phil Branch, guard
1954—Buck Lansford, tackle
1955—Menan Schriewer

ALL-STAR GAME SELECTIONS

1935—Bohn Hilliard, halfback
1938—Hugh Wolfe, halfback
1942—Mal Kutner, end
1943—Roy Dale McKay, fullback
1944—Pete Layden, fullback
1944—Roy Dale McKay, fullback
1944—Ralph Park, halfback
1945—Ralph Park, halfback
1946—Noble Doss, halfback
1946—Harold Jungmichel, guard
1947—W. Harold (Spot) Collins, guard
1948—Bobby Layne, quarterback
1948—Max Bumgardner, end
1948—Dick Harris, center
1949—George Petrovich, tackle
1951—Kenneth Jackson, tackle
*1951—Lewis (Bud) McFadin, guard
1952—Bobby Dillon, halfback
*1953—Gib Dawson, halfback
1953—Harley Sewell, guard
1954—Phi Branch, guard
*1954—Carlton Massey, end
1955—Buck Lansford, tackle
1962—James Saxton, halfback
1964—Duke Carlisle, quarterback
1964—Scott Appleton, tackle
1966—Tommy Nobis, guard
1969—Bill Bradley, back
1969—Bob McKay, tackle
1972—Jim Bertelsen, back
1973—Jerry Sisemore, tackle

* Named most valuable player.

COACHES' ALL-AMERICA GAME SELECTIONS

1962—James Saxton, back
1963—John Treadwell, linebacker; Ray Poage, back
1964—Scott Appleton, tackle
1965—Harold Philipp, back
1966—Tommy Nobis, linebacker; Phil Harris, back; Pete Lammons, end
1967—John Elliott, tackle; Gene Bledsoe, guard
1969—Bill Bradley, back
1970—Bob McKay, tackle
1971—Bobby Wuensch, tackle; Bill Atessis, end
1972—Stan Mauldin, end
1973—Jerry Sisemore, tackle
1974—Bill Wyman, center

TEXAS' RANK AMONG NATION'S TOP TEN

(Associated Press Poll)

1941—Fourth	1962—Fourth
1945—Tenth	1963—First
1947—Fifth	1964—Fifth
1950—Third	1968—Third
1952—Tenth	1969—First
1959—Fourth	1970—Third
1961—Third	1972—Third

(United Press Poll)

1950—Second	1964—Fifth
1953—Eighth	1968—Fifth
1959—Fourth	1969—First
1961—Fourth	1970—First
1962—Fourth	1972—Seventh
1963—First	

TEXAS' BOWL GAME RECORD

The University of Texas has played in 19 bowl games. The Longhorns have compiled an 11-6-2 record in such post-season contests.

Years	Bowl	Result	Site
1943	Cotton	Texas 14, Georgia Tech 7	Dallas
1944	Cotton	Texas 7, Randolph Field 7	Dallas
1946	Cotton	Texas 40, Missouri 27	Dallas
1948	Sugar	Texas 27, Alabama 7	New Orleans
1949	Orange	Texas 41, Georgia 28	Miami
1951	Cotton	Tennessee 20, Texas 14	Dallas
1953	Cotton	Texas 16, Tennessee 0	Dallas
1958	Sugar	Mississippi 39, Texas 7	New Orleans
1960	Cotton	Syracuse 23, Texas 14	Dallas
1960	Bluebonnet	Texas 3, Alabama 3	Houston
1962	Cotton	Texas 12, Mississippi 7	Dallas
1963	Cotton	LSU 13, Texas 0	Dallas
1964	Cotton	Texas 28, Navy 6	Dallas
1965	Orange	Texas 21, Alabama 17	Miami
1966	Bluebonnet	Texas 19, Mississippi 0	Houston
1969	Cotton	Texas 36, Tennessee 13	Dallas
1970	Cotton	Texas 21, Notre Dame 17	Dallas
1971	Cotton	Notre Dame 24, Texas 11	Dallas
1972	Cotton	Penn State 30, Texas 6	Dallas
1973	Cotton	Texas 17, Alabama 13	Dallas
1974	Cotton	Nebraska 19, Texas 3	Dallas

LONGHORN HALL OF HONOR

One of The University of Texas' newer—but one of its most cherished—athletic traditions is the Longhorn Hall of Honor.

The governing body, the Longhorn Hall of Honor Council, is made up exclusively of men who have lettered at The University of Texas. The Council is in charge of all arrangements for the vote of lettermen and for the installation banquet.

Mounted silver scrolls, which carry the announcement that they are presented "in recognition of those qualities that brought credit and renown to The University of Texas," are presented to the honorees.

In addition, large portraits of the honorees are hung in the beautiful Lettermen's Lounge at Memorial Stadium.

A complete list of the men enshrined in the Longhorn Hall of Honor:

1957 HONOREES
L. Theo Bellmont, deceased
William J. (Uncle Billy) Disch, deceased
Louis Jordan, deceased
Dr. Daniel A. Penick, deceased

1958 HONOREES
Gus (Pig) Dittmar
Dr. Wilson H. (Bull) Elkins
Arnold Kirkpatrick, deceased
Lutcher Stark, deceased

1959 HONOREES
Major General K. L. Berry, deceased
James A. (Pete) Edmond, deceased
George (Hook) McCullough, deceased
Harrison Stafford

1960 HONOREES
Dana X. Bible
David (Skippy) Browning, deceased
Jack Gray
Ernie Koy

1961 HONOREES
Frank "Pinky" Higgins, deceased
Pete Layden
Clyde Littlefield
Oscar Eckhardt, deceased

1962 HONOREES
Charley Coates
Jack Crain
Bibb Falk
Slater Martin

1963 HONOREES

Hub Bechtol
C. L. (Ox) Higgins, deceased

Bobby Layne
Ed Olle, deceased

1964 HONOREES

Wilmer Allison
Bohn Hilliard

Dr. Bobby Moers
A. M. G. (Swede) Swenson, deceased

1965 HONOREES

Maxey Hart
Joe Ward

Mal Kutner
Tex Robertson

1966 HONOREES

F. T. (Star) Baldwin
Harvey (Chink) Wallender

Billy (Rooster) Andrews
Gover (Ox) Emerson

1967 HONOREES

Dr. C. J. Alderson, deceased
Dr. Denton Cooley

Grady Hatton
Ed Price

1968 HONOREES

Blair Cherry, deceased
Walter W. Fisher, deceasd
James H. Hart, Sr., deceased
Charles I. Francis

H. C. Gilstrap
Dexter Shelley, deceased
Sandy Eesquivel, deceased

1969 HONOREES

Abb Curtis
Jerry Thompson
Semp Russ
Stan Mauldin, deceased

Harvey Penick
Lloyd Gregory
Alva Carlton

1970 HONOREES

Holly Brock, deceased
Chal Daniel, deceased
Bowie Duncan

Tex Hughson
Lucian Parrish, deceased
Jim Reese

1971 HONOREES

O. J. Clements
Tom Hamilton
Dick Harris

Tom Landry
W. O. Murray
Don Robinson, deceased

1972 HONOREES

Len Barrell
Gene Berry, deceased
Bobby Dillon
John Hargis

Wallace Scott, Jr.
Ed White
Lewis White

TEXAS' LARGEST MARGIN OF VICTORY
OVER CONFERENCE OPPONENTS

Arkansas	54-0 in 1894
Baylor	77-0 in 1913
Rice	59-0 in 1915
SMU	74-0 in 1916
Texas A&M	48-0 in 1898
TCU	72-0 in 1915
Texas Tech	43-0 in 1949

TEXAS FOOTBALL HISTORY

Year	Coach	Captain	Record (Won-Lost-Tied)	Pts.	Opp.
1893		James Morrison	4—0—0	98	16
1894	R. D. Wentworth (Wms.)	Victor Moore	6—1—0	191	28
1895	Frank Crawford (Neb.)	Ray McLane, Wallace Ralston	5—0—0	96	0
1896	Harry Robinson (Tufts)	P. S. Jones, Julius F. House	4—2—1	88	36
1897	W. F. Kelly (Dartmouth)	Dan Parker, Jr.	6—2—0	144	60
1898	D. F. Edwards (Prin.)	R. W. Wortham	5—1—0	136	4
1899	M. G. Clarke (Chicago)	James H. Hart	6—2—0	117	24
1900	S. H. Thompson (Prin.)	Walter Schreiner	6—0—0	113	13
1901	S. H. Thompson	M. M. McMahon	8—2—1	155	71
1902	J. B. Hart (Yale)	I. V. Duncan	6—3—1	87	40
1903	Ralph Hutchinson (Prin.)	R. G. Watson	5—1—2	131	28
1904	Ralph Hutchinson	R. G. Watson	6—2—0	219	88
1905	Ralph Hutchinson	Don Robinson	5—4—0	98	68
1906	H. R. Schenker (Yale)	L. W. Parrish	9—1—0	201	60
1907	W. E. Metzenthin (Col.)	Bowie Duncan	6—1—1	154	53
1908	W. E. Metzenthin	L. H. Feldhake	5—4—0	135	135
1909	Dexter Draper (Penn.)	Ben Dyer	4—3—1	105	50
1910	W. S. Wasmund (Mich.)	A. L. Kirkpatrick	6—2—0	157	29
1911	Dave Allerdice (Mich.)	Marshall Ramsdell	5—2—0	66	19
1912	Dave Allerdice	Frost Woodhull	7—1—0	201	62
1913	Dave Allerdice	W. C. Brown	7—1—0	250	56
1914	Dave Allerdice	Louis Jordan	8—0—0	358	21
1915	Dave Allerdice	K. L. Berry	6—3—0	335	69
1916	Eugene Van Gent (Wisc.)	Pig Dittmar	7—2—0	218	36
1917	Bill Juneau (Wisc.)	Billy Trabue	4—4—0	89	40
1918	Bill Juneau	Dave Pena	9—0—0	194	14
1919	Bill Juneau	Ghent Graves	6—3—0	181	63
1920	Berry Whitaker (Ind.)	Maxey Hart	9—0—0	282	13
1921	Berry Whitaker	Tom Dennis	6—1—1	268	27
1922	Berry Whitaker	A. M. G. Swenson	7—2—0	202	68

Year	Coach	Captain(s)	Record	PF	PA
1923	E. J. Stewart (West. Res.)	Lane Tynes	8—0—1	241	21
1924	E. J. Stewart	James Marley	5—3—1	109	64
1925	E. J. Stewart	Stuart Wright	6—2—1	157	51
1926	E. J. Stewart	Mack Saxon	5—4—0	146	69
1927	Clyde Littlefield (Texas)	Ox Higgins	6—2—1	164	73
1928	Clyde Littlefield	Rufus King	7—2—0	122	32
1929	Clyde Littlefield	Gordy Brown	5—2—2	132	28
1930	Clyde Littlefield	Dexter Shelley	8—1—1	179	20
1931	Clyde Littlefield	Dutch Baumgarten	6—4—0	131	58
1932	Clyde Littlefield	Ernie Koy, Wilson Cook	8—2—0	220	49
1933	Clyde Littlefield	Bill Smith	4—5—2	112	104
1934	Jack Chevigny (N. D.)	Bohn Hilliard, Chas. Coates	7—2—1	137	85
1935	Jack Chevigny	Joe Smartt	4—6—0	138	174
1936	Jack Chevigny	Clint Small	2—6—1	69	128
1937	Dana X Bible (Carson-Newman)		2—6—1	60	103
1938	Dana X. Bible		1—8—0	52	162
1939	Dana X. Bible	Park Myers, Ned McDonald	5—4—0	106	125
1940	Dana X. Bible	Ted Dawson, Jimmy Grubbs	8—2—0	172	77
1941	Dana X. Bible	Pete Layden	8—1—1	338	55
1942	Dana X. Bible	Wallace Scott, J. Schwarting	9—2—0	244	49
1943	Dana X. Bible	Joe Magliolo, Ralph Park, Joe Parker	7—1—1	277	54
1944	Dana X. Bible	Harold Fischer, Jack Sachse	5—4—0	119	76
1945	Dana X. Bible	Jimmy Plyler	10—1—0	257	86
1946	Dana X. Bible	Spot Collins, Audrey Gill	8—2—0	290	68
1947	Blair Cherry (TCU)	Max Bumgardner, Raymond Jones	10—1—0	292	74
1948	Blair Cherry	Tom Landry, Dick Harris	7—3—1	223	147
1949	Blair Cherry	Billy Pyle, Danny Wolfe	6—4—0	290	93
1950	Blair Cherry	Dick Rowan, Bubba Shands	9—2—0	252	148
1951	Ed Price (Texas)	Bobby Dillon, June Davis	7—3—0	182	129
1952	Ed Price	Richard Ochoa, Bill McDonald, Jack Barton	9—2—0	278	164
1953	Ed Price	Carlton Massey, Gilmer Spring, Bunny Andrews	7—3—0	190	125
1954	Ed Price	Buck Lansford, Billy Quinn, Howard Moon	4—5—1	158	161
1955	Ed Price	Herb Gray, Menan Schriewer, Johnny Tatum	5—5—0	189	212
1956	Ed Price	Mike Trant, Joe Losack, Allen Ernst, Don Maroney	1—9—0	101	272
1957	Darrell Royal (Oklahoma)	Walter Fondren, Louis Del Homme	6—4—1	159	149
1958	Darrell Royal	Arlis Parkhurst, Bob Bryant	7—3—0	157	152
1959	Darrel Royal	Don Allen, Monte Lee	9—2—0	216	96
1960	Darrell Royal	Monte Lee, Dick Jones	7—3—1	167	78
1961	Darrell Royal	Mike Cotten, Don Talbert	10—1—0	303	66
1962	Darrell Royal	Pat Culpepper, Perry McWilliams	9—1—1	184	72
1963	Darrell Royal	Scott Appleton, Tommy Ford, David McWilliams	11—0—0	243	71
1964	Darrell Royal	Jim Hudson, Tim Doerr	10—1—0	220	81
1965	Darrell Royal	Tommy Nobis, Marvin Kristynik	6—4—0	231	153
1966	Darrell Royal	Diron Talbert, John Elliott, Barney Giles	7—4—0	194	111
1967	Darrell Royal	Linus Baer, Joel Brame	6—4—0	186	123
1968	Darrell Royal	Bill Bradley, Chris Gilbert, Corby Robertson	9—1—1	379	198
1969	Darrell Royal	Ted Koy, James Street, Glen Halsell	11—0—0	435	119
1970	Darrell Royal	Steve Worster, Bobby Wuensch, Scott Henderson, Bill Zapalac	10—1—0	423	149
1971	Darrell Royal	Eddie Phillips, Tommy Woodard, Stan Mauldin, Jim Bertelsen	8—3—0	281	169
1972	Darrell Royal	Jerry Sisemore, Randy Braband, Alan Lowry	10—1—0	271	121
1973	Darrell Royal	Glen Gaspard, Bill Wyman	8-3-0	367	162

ALL-TIME STANDING OF TEXAS WITH ITS 95 OPPONENTS, 1893-1972

Opponent	First Meeting	Latest Renewal	Texas Won	Texas Lost	Ties
Alabama	1902	1972	6	0	1
Arizona	1925	1925	1	0	0
Arkansas	1894	1972	40	14	0
Army	1964	1964	1	0	0
Auburn	1910	1925	3	0	0
Austin College	1912	1923	6	0	0
Austin YMCA	1894	1895	3	0	0
Baylor	1901	1972	47	11	4
Bergstrom Field	1945	1945	1	0	0
Blackland AA Field	1943	1943	1	0	0
California	1959	1970	4	0	0
Camp Mabry Auto Sch.	1918	1918	1	0	0
Centenary	1929	1935	3	2	2
Chicago	1904	1904	0	1	0
Colorado	1940	1946	3	0	0
Colorado College	1908	1908	0	1	0
Corpus Christi NAS	1942	1942	1	0	0
Dallas Univ.	1893	1899	7	1	1
Dallas Ath. Club	1901	1901	1	0	0
Daniel Baker	1906	1932	3	0	0
Deaf School	1903	1903	1	0	0
Florida	1924	1940	2	0	1
Ft. Worth Univ.	1897	1897	1	1	0
Galveston High	1895	1898	3	0	0
Georgia	1948	1958	3	0	0
Georgia Tech	1942	1942	1	0	0
Harvard	1931	1931	0	1	0
Haskell	1902	1919	6	5	0
Houston High	1897	1901	2	0	0
Houston, U. of	1953	1968	1	0	1
Howard Payne	1919	1930	5	0	0
Idaho	1949	1949	1	0	0
Indiana	1940	1966	3	0	0
Kansas City Medics	1900	1900	1	0	0
Kansas	1901	1938	0	2	0
Kansas State	1913	1942	3	1	0
Kentucky	1951	1951	1	0	0
Kirksville	1901	1901	0	1	0
LSU	1896	1962	8	7	1
Maryland	1959	1960	2	0	0
Miami	1972	1972	1	0	0
Minnesota	1936	1936	0	1	0
Mississippi A&M	1921	1921	1	0	0
Mississippi	1912	1966	5	1	0
Missouri	1894	1946	6	4	0
Nashville	1901	1902	1	0	1
Navy	1963	1969	2	0	0
Nebraska	1933	1960	1	2	0
New Mexico	1948	1948	1	0	0
North Carolina	1947	1952	3	1	0
Northwestern	1942	1942	0	1	0
Notre Dame	1913	1971	2	5	0
Oklahoma	1900	1972	42	23	2
Okla. SW Teachers	1926	1927	2	0	0
Okla. State	1916	1968	9	1	0
Oregon	1941	1971	4	0	0
Penn State	1972	1972	0	1	0
Phillips	1919	1926	5	1	0
Polytechnic	1913	1913	1	0	0
Purdue	1950	1951	2	0	0
Radio School	1918	1918	2	0	0
Randolph Field	1943	1944	0	1	1
Ream Flying Field	1918	1918	1	0	0
Rice	1914	1972	38	20	1
St. Edwards	1921	1929	3	0	0
San Antonio	1893	1899	8	0	0

School	First	Last	W	L	T
School of Mines	1930	1933	2	0	0
Sewanee	1898	1915	4	3	0
Simmons	1920	1931	2	0	0
South Carolina	1957	1957	0	1	0
Southern California	1955	1967	0	4	0
SMU	1916	1972	29	19	4
Southwest Teachers	1930	1930	1	0	0
Southwestern	1908	1945	20	2	0
Syracuse	1959	1959	0	1	0
Temple	1949	1949	1	0	0
Tennessee	1950	1968	2	1	0
Texas A&I	1935	1935	1	0	0
Texas A&M	1894	1972	56	18	5
TCU	1897	1972	37	19	1
Texas Tech	1928	1972	19	3	0
Transylvania	1905	1910	1	1	0
Trinity	1902	1927	6	0	0
Tulane	1894	1965	15	1	1
Twenty-Sixth Infantry	1906	1906	1	0	0
UCLA	1970	1971	2	0	0
Utah State	1972	1972	1	0	0
Vanderbilt	1899	1928	3	8	1
Villanova	1953	1953	1	0	0
Wabash	1914	1914	1	0	0
Washington (of St. Louis)	1904	1906	2	0	0
Wash. State	1954	1961	2	0	0
West Texas Mil. Acad.	1906	1906	1	0	0
West Virginia	1956	1956	0	1	0
Wisconsin	1939	1939	1	0	0
TOTAL			528	192	28

LONGHORNS' S.W.C. TITLES

Year	Conference			Full Season		
	W	L	T	W	L	T
1920	5	0	0	9	0	0
1928	5	1	0	7	2	0
1930	4	1	0	8	1	1
1942	5	1	0	9	2	0
y1943	5	0	0	7	1	1
1950	6	0	0	9	2	0
1945	5	1	0	10	1	0
1952	6	0	0	9	2	0
x1953	5	1	0	7	3	0
x1959	5	1	0	9	2	0
x1961	6	1	0	10	1	0
1962	6	0	1	9	1	1
1963	7	0	0	11	0	0
x1968	6	1	0	9	1	1
1969	7	0	0	11	0	0
1970	7	0	0	10	1	0
1971	6	1	0	8	3	0
1972	7	0	0	10	1	0
1973	7	0	0	8	3	0

x—Co-champion. y—This marked first time in SWC history for school to repeat as undisputed football champion.

NOTE—Texas also had best SWC record in 1916 (5-1-0) and 1918 (4-0-0); however no championships were awarded those years.

ALL-TIME SCORES WITH INDIVIDUAL OPPONENTS
(Texas' Score Appears First in All Instances)

Alabama
1902	10- 0
1915	20- 0
1922	19-10
1947	27-7b4
1960	3-3b10
1964	21-17b14
1972	17-13b20

Won 6, Lost 0, Tied 1

Arizona
1925	20- 0

Won 1, Lost 0

Arkansas
1894	54- 0
1903	15- 0
1905	4- 0
1906	11- 0
1907	26- 6
1908	21- 0
1911	12- 0
1912	48- 0
1916	52- 0
1917	20- 0
1919	35- 7
1928	20- 7
1929	27- 0
1932	34- 0
1933	6-20
1934	19-12
1935	13-28
1936	0- 6
1937	10-21
1938	6-42
1939	14-13
1940	21- 0
1941	48-14
1942	47- 6
1943	34- 0
1944	19- 0
1945	34- 7
1946	20- 0
1947	21- 6
1948	14- 6
1949	27-14
1950	19-14
1951	14-16
1952	44- 7
1953	16- 7
1954	7-20
1955	20-27
1956	14-32
1957	17- 0
1958	24- 6
1959	13-12
1960	23-24
1961	33- 7
1962	7- 3
1963	17-13
1964	13-14
1965	24-27
1966	7-12
1967	21-12
1968	39-29
1969	15-14
1970	42- 7
1971	7-31
1972	35-15

Won 40, Lost 14

Army
1964	17- 6

Won 1, Lost 0

Auburn
1910	9- 0
1911	18- 5
1925	33- 0

Won 3, Lost 0

Austin College
1912	3- 0
1913	27- 6
1920	54- 0
1921	60- 0
1922	19- 0
1923	31- 0

Won 6, Lost 0

Austin YMCA
1894	6- 0
1894	24- 0
1895	24- 0

Won 3, Lost 0

Baylor
1901	23- 0
1903	48- 0
1904	58- 0
1905	39- 0
1907	27-11
1908	27- 5
1910	1-0*
1911	11- 0
1912	19- 7
1913	77- 0
1914	57- 0
1916	3- 7
1917	0- 3
1919	29-13
1923	7- 7
1924	10-28
1925	13- 3
1926	7-10
1927	13-12
1928	6- 0
1929	0- 0
1930	14- 0
1931	25- 0
1932	19- 0
1933	0- 3
1934	25- 6
1935	25- 6
1936	18-21
1937	9- 6
1938	3-14
1939	0-20
1940	13- 0
1941	7- 7
1942	20- 0
1945	21-14
1946	22- 7
1947	28- 7
1948	13-10
1949	20- 0
1950	27 20
1951	6-18
1952	35-33
1953	21-20
1954	7-13
1955	21-20
1956	7-10
1957	7- 7
1958	20-15
1959	13-12
1960	12- 7
1961	33- 7
1962	27-12
1963	7- 0
1964	20-14
1965	35-14
1966	26-14
1967	24- 0
1968	47-26
1969	56-14
1970	21-14
1971	24- 0
1972	17- 3

Won 47, Lost 11, Tied 4

Bergstrom Field
1945	13- 7

Won 1, Lost 0

Blackland Army Air Field
1943	65- 6

Won 1, Lost 0

California
1959	33- 0
1961	28- 3
1969	17- 0
1970	56-15

Won 4, Lost 0

Camp Mabry Auto School
1918	22- 0

Won 1, Lost 0

Centenary
1929	20- 0
1930	0- 0
1931	6- 0
1932	6-13
1933	0- 0
1934	6- 9
1935	19-13

Won 3, Lost 2, Tied 2

Chicago
1904	0-68

Won 0, Lost 1

Colorado
1940	39- 7
1941	34- 6
1946	76- 0

Won 3, Lost 0

Colorado College
1908	0-15

Won 0, Lost 1

Corpus Christi NAS
1942	40- 0

Won 1, Lost 0

Dallas Univ.
1893	18-16
1893	16- 0
1895	10- 0
1896	0- 0
1896	22- 4
1897	4-22
1897	20-16
1898	26- 0
1899	11- 6

Won 7, Lost 1, Tied 1

Dallas Athletic Club
1901	12- 0

Won 1, Lost 0

Daniel Baker
1906	40- 0
1915	92- 0
1932	26- 0

Won 3, Lost 0

Deaf School
1903	17- 0

Won 1, Lost 0

Florida
1924	7- 7
1939	12- 0
1940	26- 0

Won 2, Lost 0, Tied 1

Fort Worth Univ.
1897	0- 6
1897	38- 0

Won 1, Lost 1

Galveston
1895	8- 0
1896	42- 0
1898	17- 0

Won 3, Lost 0

*—Baylor left field because of disagreement with referee; score was tied 6-6 at the half.

Georgia
1948 .... 41–28b5
1957 .... 26– 7
1958 .... 13– 8
Won 3, Lost 0

Georgia Tech
1942 .... 14–7b1
Won 1, Lost 0

Harvard
1931 7–35
Won 0, Lost 1

Haskell
1902 0–12
1903 .... 0– 6
1904 .... 0– 4
1905 0–17
1906 .... 28– 0
1907 45–10
1909 11–12
1910 .... 68– 3
1912 .... 14– 7
1914 .... 23– 7
1919 .... 13– 7
Won 6, Lost 5

Houston High
1897 .... 42– 6
1901 .... 32– 0
Won 2, Lost 0

Univ. of Houston
1953 .... 28– 7
1968 20–20
Won 1, Lost 0, Tied 1

Howard Payne
1919 .... 26– 0
1920 .... 41– 7
1921 .... 21– 0
1924 .... 6– 0
1930 .... 26– 0
Won 5, Lost 0

Idaho
1949 .... 56– 7
Won 1, Lost 0

Indiana
1940 .... 13– 6
1965 27–12
1966 .... 35– 0
Won 3, Lost 0

Kansas City Medics
1900 .... 30– 0
Won 1, Lost 0

Univ. of Kansas
1901 0–12
1938 18–19
Won 0, Lost 2

Kansas State
1913 .... 46– 0
1926 3–13
1927 .... 41– 7
1942 .... 64– 0
Won 3, Lost 1

Kentucky
1951 .... 7– 6
Won 1, Lost 0

Kirksville
1901 0–48
Won 0, Lost 1

LSU
1896 0–14
1899 .... 29– 0
1902 .... 0– 5
1907 .... 12– 5
1910 .... 12– 6
1935 6–18
1936 .... 6– 6
1937 .... 0– 9
1938 0–20
1941 .... 34– 0
1948 .... 33– 0
1950 .... 21– 6
1952 35–14
1953 7–20
1954 .... 20– 6
1962 .... 0–13b12
Won 8, Lost 7, Tied 1

Maryland
1959 .... 26– 0
1960 .... 34– 0
Won 2, Lost 0

Miami
1972 23–10
Won 1, Lost 0

Minnesota
1936 19–47
Won 0, Lost 1

Mississippi A&M
1921 .... 54– 7
Won 1, Lost 0

Mississippi (Ole Miss)
1912 53–14
1914 .... 66– 7
1925 .... 25– 0
1957 .... 7–39b8
1961 .... 12–7b11
1966 .... 19–0b15
Won 5, Lost 1

Missouri
1894 0–28
1896 0–10
1900 17–11
1901 .... 11– 0
1907 .... 4– 5
1916 .... 0– 3
1931 .... 31– 0
1932 .... 65– 0
1945 .... 40–27b3
1946 .... 42– 0
Won 6, Lost 4

Nashville
1901 .... 5– 5
1902 .... 11– 5
Won 1, Lost 0, Tied 1

Navy
1963 .... 28–6b13
1969 56–17
Won 2, Lost 0

Nebraska
1933 0–26
1959 .... 20– 0
1960 13–14
Won 1, Lost 2

New Mexico
1948 .... 47– 0
Won 1, Lost 0

North Carolina
1947 .... 34– 0
1948 7–34
1951 45–20
1952 .... 28– 7
Won 3, Lost 1

Northwestern
1942 .... 0– 3
Won 0, Lost 1

Notre Dame
1913 7–30
1915 7–36
1934 .... 7– 6
1952 3–14
1954 0–21
1969 .... 21–17b17
1970 .... 11–24b18
Won 2, Lost 5

Univ. of Oklahoma
1900 .... 28– 2
1901 .... 12– 6
1901 .... 11– 0
1902 .... 22– 6
1903 .... 11– 5
1903 .... 6– 6
1904 40–10
1905 .... 0– 2
1906 .... 10– 9
1907 29–10
1908 0–50
1909 .... 30– 0
1910 .... 0– 3
1911 .... 3– 6
1912 6–21
1913 .... 14– 6
1914 .... 32– 7
1915 13–14
1916 .... 21– 7
1917 0–14
1919 7–12
1922 .... 32– 7
1923 26–14
1929 .... 21– 0
1930 .... 17– 7
1931 .... 3– 0
1932 17–10
1933 .... 0– 9
1934 .... 19– 0
1935 .... 12– 7
1936 .... 6– 0
1937 .... 7– 7
1938 0–13
1939 12–24
1940 19–16
1941 .... 40– 7
1942 .... 7– 0
1943 .... 13– 7
1944 .... 20– 0
1945 .... 12– 7
1946 20–13
1947 34–14
1948 14–20
1949 14–20
1950 13–14
1951 .... 9– 7
1952 20–49
1953 14–19
1954 7–14
1955 0–20
1956 0–45
1957 7–21
1958 15–14
1959 19–12
1960 .... 24– 0
1961 .... 28– 7
1962 .... 9– 6
1963 .... 28– 7
1964 .... 28– 7
1965 .... 19– 0
1966 9–18
1967 .... 9– 7
1968 26–20
1969 27–17
1970 .... 41– 9
1971 27–48
1972 0–27
Won 42, Lost 23, Tied 2

Oklahoma SW Teachers
1926 .... 31– 7
1927 .... 43– 0
Won 2, Lost 0

Oklahoma State
1916 .... 14– 6
1917 .... 7– 3
1918 .... 27– 5
1920 .... 21– 0
1922 .... 19– 7
1944 8–13
1946 .... 54– 6
1963 .... 34– 7
1967 .... 19– 0
1968 .... 31– 3
Won 9, Lost 1

Oregon
Year	Score
1941	71– 7
1947	38–13
1962	25–13
1971	35– 7

Won 4, Lost 0

Penn State
Year	Score
1972	6–31B19

Phillips
Year	Score
1919	0–10
1920	27– 0
1922	41–10
1923	51– 0
1924	27– 0
1926	27– 0

Won 5, Lost 1

Polytechnic
Year	Score
1913	14– 7

Won 1, Lost 0

Purdue
Year	Score
1950	34–26
1951	14– 6

Won 2, Lost 0

Radio School
Year	Score
1918	25– 0
1918	22– 7

Won 2, Lost 0

Randolph Field
Year	Score
1943	7–7b2
1944	6–42

Won 0, Lost 1, Tied 1

Ream Flying Field
Year	Score
1918	26– 2

Won 1, Lost 0

Rice
Year	Score
1914	41– 0
1915	59– 0
1916	16– 2
1917	0–13
1918	14– 0
1919	32– 7
1920	21– 0
1921	56– 0
1922	29– 0
1923	27– 0
1924	6–19
1925	27– 6
1926	20– 0
1927	27– 0
1928	13– 6
1929	39– 0
1930	0– 6
1931	0– 7
1932	18– 6
1933	18– 0
1934	9–20
1935	19–28
1936	0– 7
1937	7–14
1938	6–13
1939	26–12
1940	0–13
1941	40– 0
1942	12– 7
1943	58– 0
1944	0– 7
1945	6– 7
1946	13–18
1947	12– 0
1948	20– 7
1949	15–17
1950	35– 7
1951	14– 6
1952	20– 7
1953	13–18
1954	7–13
1955	32–14
1956	7–28
1957	19–14
1958	7–34
1959	28– 6
1960	0– 7
1961	34– 7
1962	14–14
1963	10– 6
1964	6– 3
1965	17–20
1966	14– 6
1967	28– 6
1968	38–14
1969	31– 0
1971	39–10
1972	45– 9

Won 38, Lost 20, Tied 1

St. Edwards
Year	Score
1921	33– 0
1928	32– 0
1929	13– 0

Won 3, Lost 0

San Antonio
Year	Score
1893	30– 0
1893	34– 0
1894	57– 0
1895	38– 0
1896	12– 4
1897	10– 0
1897	12– 0
1899	28– 0

Won 8, Lost 0

School of Mines
Year	Score
1930	28– 0
1933	22– 6

Won 2, Lost 0

Sewanee
Year	Score
1898	0– 4
1899	0–12
1902	11– 0
1905	17–10
1911	5– 6
1913	13– 7
1915	27– 6

Won 4, Lost 3

Simmons
Year	Score
1920	63– 0
1931	36– 0

Won 2, Lost 0

South Carolina
Year	Score
1957	21–27

Won 0, Lost 1

Southern California
Year	Score
1955	7–19
1956	20–44
1966	6–10
1967	13–17

Won 0, Lost 4

SMU
Year	Score
1916	74– 0
1918	32– 0
1920	21– 3
1924	6–10
1925	0– 0
1926	17–21
1927	0–14
1928	2– 6
1929	0– 0
1930	25– 7
1931	7– 9
1932	14– 6
1933	10– 0
1934	7– 7
1935	0–20
1936	7–14
1937	2–13
1938	6– 7
1939	0–10
1940	13–21
1941	34– 0
1942	21– 7
1943	20– 0
1944	34– 7
1945	12– 7
1946	19– 3
1947	13–14
1948	6–21
1949	6– 7
1950	23–20
1951	20–13
1952	31–14
1953	16– 7
1954	13–13
1955	19–18
1956	19–20
1957	12–19
1958	10–26
1959	21– 0
1960	17– 7
1961	27– 0
1962	6– 0
1963	17–12
1964	7– 0
1965	14–31
1966	12–13
1967	35–28
1968	38– 7
1969	45–14
1970	42–15
1971	22–18
1972	17– 9

Won 28, Lost 19, Tied 4

Southwest Teachers
Year	Score
1930	36– 0

Won 1, Lost 0

Southwestern
Year	Score
1908	9–11
1909	12– 0
1910	11– 6
1911	11– 2
1912	28– 3
1913	52– 0
1914	70– 0
1915	45– 0
1916	17– 3
1917	35– 0
1919	39– 0
1920	27– 0
1921	44– 0
1922	26– 0
1923	44– 0
1924	27– 0
1925	33– 0
1926	27– 6
1933	46– 0
1943	7–14
1944	20– 0
1945	46– 0

Won 20, Lost 2

Syracuse
Year	Score
1959	14–23b9

Won 0, Lost 1

Temple
Year	Score
1949	54– 0

Won 1, Lost 0

Tennessee
Year	Score
1950	14–20b6
1952	16–0b7
1968	36–13b16

Won 2, Lost 1

Texas A&I
Year	Score
1935	38– 6

Won 1, Lost 0

Texas A&M
Year	Score
1894	38– 0
1898	48– 0
1899	6– 0
1900	5– 0
1900	11– 0
1901	32– 0
1901	17– 0
1902	0–12
1902	0– 0
1903	29– 6
1904	34– 6
1905	27– 0
1906	24– 0
1907	0– 0
1907	11– 6
1908	24– 8
1908	28–12
1909	0–23
1909	0– 5
1910	8–14
1911	6– 0
1915	0–13
1916	21– 7
1917	0– 7
1918	7– 0
1919	0– 7

Year	Score
1920	7–3
1921	0–0
1922	7–14
1923	6–0
1924	7–0
1925	0–28
1926	14–5
1927	7–28
1928	19–0
1929	0–13
1930	26–0
1931	6–7
1932	21–0
1933	10–10
1934	13–0
1935	6–20
1936	7–0
1937	0–7
1938	7–6
1939	0–20
1940	7–0
1941	23–0
1942	12–6
1943	27–13
1944	6–0
1945	20–10
1946	24–7
1947	32–13
1948	14–14
1949	42–14
1950	17–0
1951	21–22
1952	32–12
1953	21–12
1954	22–13
1955	21–6
1956	21–34
1957	9–7
1958	27–0
1959	20–17
1960	21–14
1961	25–0
1962	13–3
1963	15–13
1964	26–7
1965	21–17
1966	22–14
1967	7–10
1968	35–14
1969	49–12
1970	52–14
1971	34–14
1972	38–3

Won 56, Lost 18, Tied 5

TCU

Year	Score
1897	18–10
1898	16–0
1898	29–0
1904	40–0
1905	11–0
1906	22–0
1908	11–6
1909	24–0
1912	30–10
1915	72–0
1918	19–0
1924	13–0
1927	0–0
1928	6–0
1929	12–15
1930	7–0
1931	10–0
1932	0–14
1933	0–30
1934	20–19
1935	0–28
1936	6–27
1937	0–14
1938	6–28
1939	25–19
1940	21–14
1941	7–14
1942	7–13
1943	46–7
1944	6–7
1945	20–0
1946	0–14
1947	20–0
1948	14–7
1949	13–14
1950	21–7
1951	32–21
1952	14–7
1953	13–3
1954	35–34
1955	20–47
1956	0–46
1957	14–2
1958	8–22
1959	9–14
1960	3–2
1961	0–6
1962	14–0
1963	17–0
1964	28–13
1965	10–25
1966	13–3
1967	17–24
1968	47–21
1969	69–7
1970	58–0
1971	31–0
1972	27–0

Won 38, Lost 19, Tied 1

Texas Tech

Year	Score
1928	12–0
1934	12–6
1937	25–12
1945	33–0
1947	33–0
1949	43–0
1950	28–14
1955	14–20
1958	12–7
1960	17–0
1961	42–14
1962	34–0
1963	49–7
1964	23–0
1965	33–7
1966	31–21
1967	13–19
1968	22–31
1969	49–7
1970	35–13
1971	28–0
1972	25–20

Won 19, Lost 3

Transylvania

Year	Score
1905	0–6
1910	48–0

Won 1, Lost 1

Trinity

Year	Score
1902	27–0
1904	24–0
1909	18–0
1912	30–0
1917	27–0
1927	20–6

Won 6, Lost 0

Tulane

Year	Score
1894	12–0
1895	16–0
1896	12–4
1899	32–0
1899	11–0
1902	6–0
1908	15–28
1909	10–10
1923	33–0
1955	35–21
1956	7–6
1957	20–6
1958	21–20
1962	35–8
1963	21–0
1964	31–0
1965	31–0

Won 15, Lost 1, Tied 1

Twenty-sixth Infantry

Year	Score
1906	21–0

Won 1, Lost 0

UCLA

Year	Score
1970	20–17
1971	28–10

Won 2, Lost 0

Utah State

Year	Score
1972	27–12

Won 1, Lost 0

Vanderbilt

Year	Score
1899	0–6
1900	22–0
1903	5–5
1905	0–33
1906	0–45
1921	0–20
1922	10–20
1923	16–0
1925	6–14
1926	0–7
1927	13–6
1928	12–13

Won 3, Lost 8, Tied 1

Villanova

Year	Score
1953	41–12

Won 1, Lost 0

Wabash

Year	Score
1914	39–0

Won 1, Lost 0

Washington (St. Louis)

Won 2, Lost 0

Year	Score
1904	23–0
1906	17–0

Washington State

Year	Score
1954	40–14
1961	41–8

Won 2, Lost 0

West Texas Military Academy

Year	Score
1906	28–0

Won 1, Lost 0

West Virginia	Wisconsin	Totals
1956 .... 6– 7	1939 .... 17– 7	Games Played: 748
Won 0, Lost 1	Won 1, Lost 0	Games Won: 528
		Games Lost: 192
		Games Tied: 28

b1—Cotton Bowl game Jan. 1, 1943.
b2—Cotton Bowl game Jan. 1, 1944.
b3—Cotton Bowl game Jan. 1, 1946.
b4—Sugar Bowl game Jan. 1, 1948.
b5—Orange Bowl game Jan. 1, 1949.
b6—Cotton Bowl game Jan. 1, 1951.
b7—Cotton Bowl game Jan. 1, 1953.
b8—Sugar Bowl game Jan. 1, 1958.
b9—Cotton Bowl game Jan. 1, 1960.
b10—Bluebonnet Bowl game Dec. 17, 1960.
b11—Cotton Bowl game Jan. 1, 1962.
b12—Cotton Bowl game Jan. 1, 1963.
b13—Cotton Bowl game Jan. 1, 1964.
b14—Orange Bowl game Jan. 1, 1965.
b15—Bluebonnet Bowl game Dec. 17, 1966
b16—**Cotton Bowl game Jan. 1, 1969**
b17—Cotton Bowl game Jan. 1, 1970
b18—Cotton Bowl game Jan. 1, 1971
b19—Cotton Bowl game Jan. 1, 1972
b20—Cotton Bowl game Jan. 1, 1973

TEXAS' ALL-TIME RECORD

*Home Games at Austin.

1893
18 Dallas 16
30 *San Antonio 0
34 *San Antonio 0
16 *Dallas 0

1894
38 *Texas Aggies 0
12 *Tulane 0
6   *Austin YMCA 0
24 *Austin YMCA 0
54 *Arkansas 0
57 San Antonio 0
0   *Missouri 28

1895
10 Dallas 0
24 *Austin YMCA 0
16 *Tulane 0
38 *San Antonio 0
8   *Galveston 0

1896
42 *Galveston 0
0   Dallas 0
12 *San Antonio 4
12 Tulane 4
0   LSU 14
22 *Dallas 4
0   *Missouri 10

1897
10 *San Antonio 0
4   Dallas 22
0   Ft. Worth 6
18 Add Ran† 10
42 *Houston 6
12 San Antonio 0
38 *Ft. Worth 0
20 *Dallas 16
    † Now TCU.

1898
16 Add Ran 0
48 *Texas Aggies 0
17 *Galveston 0
29 *Add Ran 0
0   *Sewanee 4
26 *Dallas 0

1899
11 Dallas 6
28 *San Antonio 0
6   Texas Aggies 0
0   *Sewanee 12
0   Vanderbilt 6
11 Tulane 0
32 *Tulane 0
29 *LSU 0

1900
28 *Oklahoma 2
22 Vanderbilt 0
5   Texas Aggies 0
17 *Missouri 11
30 *Kans. City Meds ... 0
11 *Texas Aggies 0

1901
32 *Houston 0
5   Nashville U. 5
12 *Oklahoma 6
17 Texas Aggies 0
23 Baylor 0
12 *Dallas AC 0
11 Missouri 0
0   Kirksville 48
0   Kansas 12
11 Oklahoma 0
32 *Texas Aggies 0

1902
22 *Oklahoma 6
11 Sewanee 0
0   LSU 5
0   Texas Aggies 0
27 *Trinity 0
0   *Haskell 12
11 Nashville U. 5
10 Alabama 0
6   Tulane 0
0   *Texas Aggies 12

1903
17 *School for Deaf 0
0   Haskell 6
6   *Oklahoma 6
48 *Baylor 0
15 *Arkansas 0
5   *Vanderbilt 5
11 Oklahoma 5
29 *Texas Aggies 6

1904
40 *TCU 0
24 *Trinity 0
0   *Haskell 4
23 Washington (St. L.) 0
0   Chicago 68
40 *Oklahoma 10
58 *Baylor 0
34 *Texas Aggies 6

1905
11 *TCU 0
0   *Haskell 17
39 *Baylor 0
0   Vanderbilt 33
4   Arkansas 0
0   Oklahoma 2
0   *Transylvania 6
17 *Sewanee 10
27 *Texas Aggies 0

1906
21 *26th Infantry 0
22 *TCU 0
28 *WTMA 0
0   Vanderbilt 45
11 Arkansas 0
10 Oklahoma 9
28 *Haskell 0
40 *Daniel Baker 0
17 *Washington (St. L.) 6
24 *Texas Aggies 0

1907
- 0 Texas Aggies 0
- 12 *LSU 5
- 15 *Haskell 10
- 26 Arkansas 6
- 4 Missouri 5
- 27 *Baylor 11
- 29 *Oklahoma 10
- 11 *Texas Aggies 6

1908
- 11 *TCU 6
- 27 *Baylor 5
- 0 *Colorado Coll. 15
- 21 *Arkansas 0
- 9 *Southwestern 11
- 24 Texas Aggies 8
- 0 Oklahoma 50
- 15 *Tulane 28
- 28 *Texas Aggies 12

1909
- 12 *Southwestern 0
- 11 Haskell 12
- 18 *Trinity 0
- 24 *TCU 0
- 0 Texas Aggies 23
- 10 Tulane 10
- 30 *Oklahoma 0
- 0 *Texas Aggies 5

1910
- 11 *Southwestern 6
- 68 *Haskell 3
- 48 *Transylvania 0
- 9 *Auburn 0
- 1 Baylor 0
- 8 Texas Aggies 14
- 12 *LSU 0
- 0 *Oklahoma 3

1911
- 11 *Southwestern 2
- 11 *Baylor 0
- 12 *Arkansas 0
- 5 *Sewanee 6
- 6 Texas Aggies 0
- 18 *Auburn 5
- 3 *Oklahoma 6

1912
- 30 *TCU 10
- 3 *Austin College 0
- 6 Oklahoma 21
- 14 *Haskell 7
- 19 Baylor 7
- 53 Mississippi 14
- 28 *Southwestern 3
- 48 *Arkansas 0

1913
- 14 *Polytechnic 7
- 27 *Austin College 6
- 77 *Baylor 0
- 13 Sewanee 7
- 52 *Southwestern 0
- 14 Oklahoma 6
- 46 *Kansas Aggies 0
- 7 *Notre Dame 30

1914
- 30 *Trinity 0
- 57 *Baylor 0
- 41 *Rice 0
- 32 Oklahoma 7
- 70 *Southwestern 0
- 23 Haskell 7
- 66 *Mississippi 7
- 39 *Wabash 0

1915
- 72 *TCU 0
- 92 *Daniel Baker 0
- 59 *Rice 0
- 13 Oklahoma 14
- 45 *Southwestern 0
- 27 Sewanee 6
- 20 *Alabama 0
- 0 Texas Aggies 13
- 7 *Notre Dame 36

1916
- 74 *SMU 0
- 16 *Rice 2
- 14 Oklahoma A&M 6
- 21 Oklahoma 7
- 3 *Baylor 7
- 0 Missouri 3
- 52 *Arkansas 0
- 17 *Southwestern 3
- 21 *Texas Aggies 7

1917
- 27 *Trinity 0
- 35 *Southwestern 0
- 0 Oklahoma 14
- 0 *Rice 13
- 0 Baylor 3
- 7 *Oklahoma A&M 3
- 0 Texas Aggies 7
- 20 *Arkansas 0

1918
- 19 *TCU 0
- 25 *Radio School 0
- 22 *Radio School 7
- 26 *Ream Flying Field 2
- 27 *Oklahoma A&M 5
- 22 *Auto Mech. Sch'l 0
- 14 Rice 0
- 32 *SMU 0
- 7 *Texas Aggies 0

1919
- 26 *Howard Payne 0
- 39 *Southwestern 0
- 0 *Phillips 10
- 7 Oklahoma 12
- 29 *Baylor 13
- 32 *Rice 7
- 35 *Arkansas 7
- 13 *Haskell 7
- 0 Texas Aggies 7

1920
- 63 *Simmons 0
- 27 *Southwestern 0
- 41 *Howard Payne 7
- 21 Oklahoma A&M 0
- 54 *Austin College 0
- 21 Rice 0
- 27 *Phillips 0
- 21 *SMU 3
- 7 *Texas Aggies 3

1921
- 33 *St. Edwards 0
- 60 *Austin College 0
- 21 *Howard Payne 0
- 0 Vanderbilt 20
- 56 *Rice 0
- 44 *Southwestern 0
- 54 *Mississippi A&M 7
- 0 Texas Aggies 0

1922
- 19 *Austin College 0
- 41 *Phillips 10
- 19 *Oklahoma A&M 7
- 10 Vanderbilt 20
- 19 *Alabama 10
- 29 Rice 0
- 26 *Southwestern 0
- 32 Oklahoma 7
- 7 *Texas Aggies 14

1923
- 31 *Austin College 0
- 51 *Phillips 0
- 33 *Tulane 0
- 16 Vanderbilt 0
- 44 *Southwestern 0
- 27 *Rice 0
- 7 Baylor 7
- 26 *Oklahoma 14
- 6 Texas Aggies 0

1924
- 27 *Southwestern 0
- 27 *Phillips 0
- 6 *Howard Payne 0
- 6 SMU 10
- 7 *Florida 7
- 6 Rice 19
- 10 *Baylor 28
- 13 TCU 0
- 7 *Texas Aggies 0

1925
- 33 *Southwestern 0
- 25 *Mississippi 0
- 6 Vanderbilt 14
- 33 Auburn 0
- 27 *Rice 6
- 0 SMU 0
- 13 *Baylor 3
- 20 *Arizona 0
- 0 Texas Aggies 28

1926
- 31 *S.W.Tchrs. (Okla.) 7
- 3 Kansas A&M 13
- 27 *Phillips 0
- 0 Vanderbilt 7
- 20 Rice 0
- 17 *SMU 21
- 7 Baylor 10
- 27 *Southwestern 6
- 14 *Texas Aggies 5

1927
- 43 *Oklahoma Tchrs. 0
- 0 *TCU 0
- 20 *Trinity 6
- 13 Vanderbilt 6
- 27 *Rice 0
- 0 SMU 14
- 13 *Baylor 12
- 41 *Kansas A&M 7
- 7 Texas Aggies 28

1928
- 32 *St. Edwards 0
- 12 *Texas Tech 0
- 12 Vanderbilt 13
- 20 *Arkansas 7
- 13 Rice 6
- 2 *SMU 6
- 6 Baylor 0
- 6 TCU 0
- 19 *Texas Aggies 0

1929
- 13 *St. Edwards 0
- 20 *Centenary 0
- 27 Arkansas 0
- 21 Oklahoma 0
- 39 *Rice 0
- 0 SMU 0
- 0 *Baylor 0
- 12 *TCU 15
- 0 Texas Aggies 13

211

1930
36 *San Marcos Tchrs. 0
28 *College of Mines 0
0 *Centenary 0
26 *Howard Payne 0
17 Oklahoma 7
0 Rice 6
25 *SMU 7
14 Baylor 0
7 TCU 0
26 *Texas Aggies 0

1931
36 *Simmons 0
31 *Missouri 0
0 *Rice 7
3 Oklahoma 0
7 Harvard 35
7 SMU 9
25 *Baylor 0
10 *TCU 0
6 Centenary 0
6 Texas Aggies 7

1932
26 *Daniel Baker 0
6 *Centenary 13
65 Missouri 0
17 Oklahoma 10
18 Rice 6
14 *SMU 6
19 Baylor 0
0 TCU 14
34 Arkansas 0
21 *Texas Aggies 0

1933
46 Southwestern 0
22 *College of Mines 6
0 Nebraska 26
0 Oklahoma 9
0 Centenary 0
18 *Rice 0
10 SMU 0
0 *Baylor 3
0 *TCU 30
6 *Arkansas 20
10 Texas Aggies 10

1934
12 Texas Tech 6
7 Notre Dame 6
19 Oklahoma 0
6 *Centenary 9
9 Rice 20
7 *SMU 7
25 *Baylor 6
20 TCU 19
19 Arkansas 12
13 *Texas Aggies 0

1935
38 *Texas A&I 6
6 LSU 18
12 Oklahoma 7
19 *Centenary 13
19 *Rice 28
0 SMU 20
25 Baylor 0
0 *TCU 28
13 *Arkansas 28
6 Texas Aggies 20

1936
6 *LSU 6
6 Oklahoma 0
18 *Baylor 21
0 Rice 7
7 *SMU 14
6 TCU 27
19 Minnesota 47
7 *Texas Aggies 0
0 Arkansas 6

1937
25 *Texas Tech 12
0 LSU 9
7 Oklahoma 7
10 *Arkansas 21
7 *Rice 14
2 SMU 13
9 Baylor 6
0 *TCU 14
0 Texas Aggies 7

1938
18 Kansas 19
0 *LSU 20
0 Oklahoma 13
0 Arkansas 42
6 Rice 13
6 *SMU 7
3 *Baylor 14
6 TCU 28
7 *Texas Aggies 6

1939
12 *Florida 0
17 Wisconsin 7
12 Oklahoma 24
14 *Arkansas 13
26 *Rice 12
0 SMU 10
0 Baylor 20
25 *TCU 19
0 Texas Aggies 20

1940
39 *Colorado 7
13 Indiana 6
19 Oklahoma 16
21 Arkansas 0
0 Rice 13
13 *SMU 21
13 *Baylor 0
21 TCU 14
7 *Texas Aggies 0
26 Florida 0

1941
34 Colorado 6
34 *LSU 0
40 Oklahoma 7
48 *Arkansas 14
40 *Rice 0
34 SMU 0
7 Baylor 7
7 *TCU 14
23 Texas Aggies 0
71 *Oregon 7

1942
40 *Corpus Christi NAS 0
64 *Kansas State 0
0 Northwestern 3
7 Oklahoma 0
47 Arkansas 6
12 Rice 7
21 *SMU 7
20 *Baylor 0
7 TCU 13
12 *Texas Aggies 6
(Cotton Bowl)
14 Georgia Tech 7

1943
65 *Blackland AAF 6
7 *Southwestern 14
13 Oklahoma 7
34 *Arkansas 0
58 *Rice 0
20 SMU 0
46 *TCU 7
27 Texas Aggies 13
(Cotton Bowl)
7 Randolph Field 7

1944
20 *Southwestern 0
6 *Randolph Field 42
20 Arkansas 0
19 Rice 7
34 *SMU 7
8 *Oklahoma A&M 13
6 TCU 7
6 *Texas Aggies 0

1945
13 *Bergstrom Field 7
46 *Southwestern 0
33 *Texas Tech 0
12 Oklahoma 7
34 Arkansas 7
6 *Rice 7
12 SMU 7
21 *Baylor 14
20 *TCU 0
20 Texas Aggies 10
(Cotton Bowl)
40 Missouri 27

1946
42 *Missouri 0
76 *Colorado 0
54 *Oklahoma A&M 6
20 Oklahoma 13
10 *Arkansas 0
13 Rice 18
19 *SMU 3
22 Baylor 7
0 TCU 14
24 *Texas Aggies 7

1947
33 *Texas Tech 0
38 Oregon 13
34 *North Carolina 0
34 Oklahoma 14
21 Arkansas 6
12 *Rice 0
13 SMU 14
28 *Baylor 7
20 *TCU 0
32 Texas Aggies 13
(Sugar Bowl)
27 Alabama 7

1948
33 *LSU 0
7 North Carolina 34
47 *New Mexico 0
14 Oklahoma 20
14 *Arkansas 6
20 Rice 7
6 *SMU 21
13 Baylor 10
14 TCU 7
14 *Texas Aggies 14
(Orange Bowl)
41 Georgia 28

212

1949
- 43 *Texas Tech 0
- 54 Temple 0
- 56 *Idaho 7
- 14 Oklahoma 20
- 27 Arkansas 14
- 15 *Rice 17
- 6 SMU 7
- 20 *Baylor 0
- 13 *TCU 14
- 42 Texas Aggies 14

1950
- 28 Texas Tech 14
- 34 *Purdue 26
- 13 Oklahoma 14
- 19 *Arkansas 14
- 35 Rice 7
- 23 *SMU 20
- 27 Baylor 20
- 21 TCU 7
- 17 *Texas Aggies 0
- 21 *LSU 6
 (Cotton Bowl)
- 14 Tennessee 20

1951
- 7 *Kentucky 6
- 14 Purdue 0
- 45 *North Carolina 20
- 9 Oklahoma 7
- 14 Arkansas 16
- 14 *Rice 6
- 20 SMU 13
- 6 *Baylor 18
- 32 *TCU 21
- 21 Texas A&M 22

1952
- 35 LSU 14
- 28 North Carolina 7
- 3 *Notre Dame 14
- 20 Oklahoma 49
- 44 *Arkansas 7
- 20 Rice 7
- 31 *SMU 14
- 35 Baylor 33
- 14 TCU 7
- 32 *Texas A&M 12
 (Cotton Bowl)
- 16 Tennessee 0

1953
- 7 LSU 20
- 41 *Villanova 12
- 28 *Houston 7
- 14 Oklahoma 19
- 16 Arkansas 7
- 13 *Rice 18
- 16 SMU 7
- 21 *Baylor 20
- 13 *TCU 3
- 21 Texas A&M 12

1954
- 20 *LSU 6
- 0 Notre Dame 21
- 40 *Wash. State 14
- 7 Oklahoma 14
- 7 *Arkansas 20
- 7 Rice 13
- 13 *SMU 13
- 7 Baylor 13
- 35 TCU 34
- 22 *Texas A&M 13

1955
- 14 *Texas Tech 20
- 35 *Tulane 21
- 7 USC 19
- 0 Oklahoma 20
- 20 Arkansas 27
- 32 *Rice 14
- 19 SMU 18
- 21 *Baylor 20
- 20 *TCU 47
- 21 Texas A&M 6

1956
- 20 *USC 44
- 7 Tulane 6
- 6 *West Virginia 7
- 0 Oklahoma 45
- 14 *Arkansas 32
- 7 Rice 28
- 19 *SMU 20
- 7 Baylor 10
- 0 TCU 46
- 21 *Texas A&M 34

1957
- 26 Georgia 7
- 20 *Tulane 6
- 21 *South Carolina 27
- 7 Oklahoma 21
- 17 Arkansas 0
- 19 *Rice 14
- 12 SMU 19
- 7 *Baylor 7
- 14 *TCU 2
- 9 Texas A&M 7
 (Sugar Bowl)
- 7 Mississippi 39

1958
- 13 *Georgia 8
- 21 Tulane 20
- 12 *Texas Tech 7
- 15 Oklahoma 14
- 24 *Arkansas 6
- 7 Rice 34
- 10 *SMU 26
- 20 Baylor 15
- 8 TCU 22
- 27 *Texas A&M 0

1959
- 20 Nebraska 0
- 26 *Maryland 0
- 33 *California 0
- 19 Oklahoma 12
- 13 Arkansas 12
- 28 *Rice 6
- 21 SMU 0
- 13 *Baylor 12
- 9 *TCU 14
- 20 Texas A&M 17
 (Cotton Bowl)
- 14 Syracuse 23

1960
- 13 *Nebraska 14
- 34 Maryland 0
- 17 *Texas Tech 0
- 24 Oklahoma 0
- 23 *Arkansas 24
- 0 Rice 7
- 17 *SMU 7
- 12 Baylor 7
- 3 TCU 2
- 21 *Texas A&M 14
 (Bluebonnet Bowl)
- 3 Alabama 3

1961
- 28 California 3
- 42 *Texas Tech 14
- 41 *Washington State 8
- 28 Oklahoma 7
- 33 Arkansas 7
- 34 *Rice 7

1962
- 25 *Oregon 13
- 34 Texas Tech 0
- 35 *Tulane 8
- 9 Oklahoma 6
- 7 *Arkansas 3
- 14 Rice 14
- 6 *SMU 0
- 27 Baylor 12
- 14 TCU 0
- 13 *Texas A&M 3
 (Cotton Bowl)
- 0 LSU 13

1963
- 21 Tulane 0
- 49 *Texas Tech 7
- 34 *Oklahoma State 7
- 28 Oklahoma 7
- 17 Arkansas 13
- 10 *Rice 6
- 17 SMU 12
- 7 *Baylor 0
- 17 *TCU 0
- 15 Texas A&M 13
 (Cotton Bowl)
- 28 Navy 6

1964
- 31 *Tulane 0
- 23 Texas Tech 0
- 17 *Army 6
- 28 Oklahoma 7
- 13 *Arkansas 14
- 6 Rice 3
- 7 *SMU 0
- 20 Baylor 14
- 28 TCU 13
- 26 *Texas A&M 7
 (Orange Bowl)
- 21 Alabama 17

1965
- 31*†Tulane 0
- 33 *Texas Tech 7
- 27 *Indiana 12
- 19 Oklahoma 0
- 24 Arkansas 27
- 17 *Rice 20
- 14 SMU 31
- 35 *Baylor 14
- 10 *TCU 25
- 21 Texas A&M 17

1966
- 6 *Sou. Calif. 10
- 31 Texas Tech 21
- 35 *Indiana 0
- 9 Oklahoma 18
- 7 *Arkansas 12
- 14 Rice 6
- 12 *SMU 13
- 26 Baylor 14
- 13 TCU 3
- 22 *Texas A&M 14
 (Bluebonnet Bowl)
- 19 Mississippi 0

1967
- 13 Sou. Calif. 17
- 13 *Texas Tech 19
- 19 *Okla. State 0
- 9 Oklahoma 7
- 21 Arkansas 12
- 14 *Rice 6
- 35 SMU 28
- 24 *Baylor 0
- 17 *TCU 24
- 7 Texas A&M 10

213

1968
- 20 *Houston 20
- 22 Texas Tech 31
- 31 *Okla. State 3
- 26 Oklahoma 20
- 39 *Arkansas 29
- 38 Rice 14
- 38 *SMU 7
- 47 Baylor 26
- 47 TCU 21
- 35 *Texas A&M 14
  (Cotton Bowl)
- 36 Tennessee 13

1969
- 17 California 0
- 9 *Texas Tech 7
- 56 *Navy 17
- 27 Oklahoma 17
- 31 *Rice 7
- 45 SMU 14
- 56 *Baylor 14
- 69 *TCU 7
- 49 Texas A&M 12
- 15 Arkansas 14
- 21 Notre Dame 17
  (Cotton Bowl)

1970
- 56 *California 15

(1968 col 2)
- 35 Texas Tech 13
- 20 *UCLA 17
- 41 Oklahoma 9
- 45 Rice 21
- 42 *SMU 15
- 21 Baylor 14
- 58 TCU 0
- 52 *Texas A&M 14
- 42 *Arkansas 7
- 11 Notre Dame 24
  (Cotton Bowl)

1971
- 28 UCLA 10
- 28 *Texas Tech 0
- 35 *Oregon 7
- 27 Oklahoma 48
- 7 Arkansas 31
- 39 *Rice 10
- 22 SMU 18
- 24 *Baylor 0
- 31 *TCU 0
- 34 *Texas A&M 14
- 6 Penn State 31
  (Cotton Bowl)

1972
- 23 *Miami 10
- 25 Texas Tech 20
- 27 *Utah State 12
- 0 Oklahoma 27
- 35 *Arkansas 15
- 45 Rice 9
- 17 *SMU 9
- 17 Baylor 3
- 27 TCU 0
- 38 *Texas A&M 3
- 17 Alabama 13
  (Cotton Bowl)

1973
- 15 Miami 20
- 28 Texas Tech 12
- 41 Wake Forest 0
- 13 Oklahoma 52
- 34 Arkansas 6
- 55 Rice 13
- 42 SMU 14
- 42 Baylor 6
- 52 TCU 7
- 42 Texas A&M 13
- 3 Nebraska 19
  (Cotton Bowl)

† Game moved to Austin after hurricane at New Orleans.

UNIVERSITY OF TEXAS LETTERMEN

"A"

Abbott, Danny G. '66, '67, '68
Aboussie, Joe '73
Achilles, James E., Jr. '68, '69, '70
Acree, S. F. '95, '96
Adams, Dan '73
Adams, Grover C. '06, '07
Adams, John Q. '49, '50, '51
Adams, Sidney M. '03
Akins, Marty '73
Aldridge, Denny C. '66, '67, '68
Alford, Parker '73
Allen, Ben '24
Allen, Don R. '57, '58, '59
Allen, George E. '52
Allen, H. K. '45
Allen, J. R. '25, '26, '27
Allinson, J. Burchell '37
Allred, John B., Jr. '49
Alvis, Roy M. '57
Amaya, Rene '73
Anderson, George W. (Mgr.) '16
Anderson, Henry G. '57, '58, '60
Anderson, Leroy E. '44
Andrews, John B. '52, '53
Andrews, William E. (Mgr.) '42, '45
Anglin, Kenneth W. '52
Appleton, Gordon S. '61, '62, '63
Arledge, David '69, '70, '71
Arnold, Jay '33, '35, '36
Arnold, Jay '71, '72, '73
Arnold, Joe E. '49, '50
Asaff, Tommy '69
Ashby, Joe B., Jr. (Mgr.) '51
Atchison, Judson '35, '36, '37
Atessis, William J. '68, '69, '70
Austin, Tom A. '16

"B"

Baebel, A. K. '33, '34
Baer, Linus L. '65, '66, '67
Bailey, Cullen W. '09
Bain, William W. (Mgr.) '35
Baines, Roy '37, '38
Baker, Charles A. '56
Baker, Danny '72
Baker, Kelly L. '65, '66
Baldridge, Robert, Jr. '31
Baldwin, J. Leo '25, '27, '28
Ballew, David '70
Bankhead, Charles '31, '32
Barclay, John A. '08, '09
Barnes, James K. '09
Barnes, John W. '66
Barrell, Leonard C. '11, '12, '13, '14
Barry, William D. '20
Bartek, David '73
Barton, A. M. (Mgr.) '02
Barton, Don R. '50, '51
Barton, Jack L. '50, '51, '52
Barton, Ray A. '60
Basey, V. D. '39, '40
Bass, Gaddis, '13
Bass, George '61, '62

215

Bauman, Edwin R. '49
Baumgardner, Joe W. '45, '46
Baumgartner, Maurice '29, '30, '31
Bayer, Mike '70, '71, '72
Beall, Jack '16
Beard, Jim '29
Beasley, Fred R. '32, '33, '34
Beaty, Curtis '27, '28, '29
Bechtol, Hubert E. '44, '45, '46
Bednarski, Fred, Jr. '58
Bedrick, Frank J. '63, '64, '65
Bell, S. Maxie '44, '45
Bennett, Charles D. '93, '94
Bennett, Lonnie '71, '72, '73
Bergen, Lawrence J. (Mgr.) '60
Berry, Eugene R. '12, '13
Berry, K. L. '12, '14, '15, '24
Bertelsen, Jim '69, '70, '71
Besselman, James A. '62, '63
Bethea, Cade '97, '98, '99
Bethea, Lamar '96, '97, '98
Beular, Ed '27, '28, '29
Bewley, E. E. '00, '01, '02
Bibby, Dause L. '31, '32
Bible, William D. '53
Birdwell, Thomas '31, '32
Birge, W. S. '11, '13, '14, '15
Bizzell, Joe B. '73
Blacklock, A. G. '97
Blaine, Robert M. '15, '16, '19
Blanch, George C. '57, '58, '59
Bland, D. C. '09, '10, '11
Blanton, Claude '30, '31, '32
Bledsoe, Hoyt E., Jr. '64, '65, '66

Blocker, William B. '04, '05
Blount, Ralph E. '45, '47, '48
Bluestein, Edwin '22, '23
Boecker, John '73
Bohn, William H. (Mgr.) '50
Bolin, Daniel P. '43, '44
Bolton, Jerrell '70, '71
Bond, Walter B. '54
Boothe, Terry '67
Borneman, Raymond T. '48, '49
Bowen, W. J. '03
Boyer, J. Wesley '37, '38
Boyles, James M. '27
Boynton, F. Y. '16
Braband, Randy '70, '71, '72
Bradford, Dewey '17
Bradley, William C. '66, '67, '68
Bralley, F. M. '22, '23
Braly, Clifford '30, '31, '32
Brame, Joel L. '65, '66, '67
Branch, Clair M. '56, '58, '59
Branch, Joseph P. '51, '52, '53
Bray, Clarence V. '61, '62, '63
Brechtel, Fred C. '45
Brennan, William W. '17, '19
Brewer, Charles N. '53, '54, '55
Brewton, Dallas P. (Mgr.) '49
Brooks, Leonard Leo, Jr. '67, '68, '69
Brown, Andrew '30, '31
Brown, Ben '21, '22
Brown, Clinton G. '01
Brown, Garry '64
Brown, Gordon A. '27, '28, '29
Brown, J. Leonard '00, '01
Brown, Samuel L. (Mgr.) '36
Brown, W. Clark '10, '12, '13

Brucks, George L. '61, '62, '63
Bryan, B. F. '37, '38
Bryant, Robert E. '56, '57, '58
Buchanan, E. L. '94
Buck, Shelby '38, '39
Buckalew, Charles O. '62, '63, '64
Bumgardner, Max A. '42, '46, '47
Burnett, McCollum, Jr. '28, '29
Burns, Richard F. '21, '22, '23
Burr, Jimmie '31, '32
Burrisk, Don '71, '72
Butler, Edmond F. '43
Buxkemper, Jerome J. '45
Byrd, Joseph H. '99

• "C"

Caldwell, Bellard '05, '06, '07
Callahan, James R. '43
Callan, Sam W. '45
Callison, Robert E. '68, '69, '71
Cameron, Donald '98
Cameron, Dougal A. '52, '53
Camp, Alex '95
Campbell, Dean '70, '71
Campbell, Paul E. '48, '49
Campbell, Thomas H. '68, '69
Campbell, William M. '68, '69
Canady, James M. '43, '46, '47
Cannon, Bruce '71, '72, '73
Cannon, David C. (Bobby) '19
Caperton, James R. '95, '96
Carlisle, Emmett A. (Duke) '61, '62, '63
Carlton, Alva '13, '14, '15, '16
Carrico, William R. '56
Cartwright, Lon D., Jr. (Mgr.) '23

Cartwright, T. Joiner (Mgr.) '20
Casey, Henry J. '16
Castleberry, Vance L. '56
Chapman, C. Moreland '34, '35
Cheatham, Frank '29
Childress, R. J. '70, '72
Choate, Leonard (Mgr.) '34
Clarke, James S. '95, '96, '97
Clay, Randall '47, '48, '49
Clayborn, Raymond '73
Clements, Joseph S. '55, '56, '57
Clewis, Howard '30, '31, '32
Coates, Charles S. '32, '33, '34
Cobb, George L. '68, '69
Cohenour, Donald '40, '41
Coit, John C. '22
Cole, Brady (Mgr.) '21
Cole, Christopher C. '99
Coleman, Joseph R. '43
Collie, Michael B. '35
Collins, Jack A. '59, '60, '61
Collins, Jack A., Sr. '34, '35, '36
Collins, Terry '69, '70
Collins, W. H. '18
Collins, William H. (Spot) '41, '42, '46
Comer, William D. '67, '68, '70
Conley, Charlie G. '16, '17, '18
Conoly, William Z. '41, '42
Conway, David '64, '65, '66
Cook, H. Wilson '30, '31, '32
Cook, Jerry C. '60, '61, '62
Cook, John A. '60, '61
Cooke, James (Mgr.) '69
Cooledge, Roy L. '31, '32
Cooper, Larry G. '58, '59, '60

Cormier, Jay '69
Cotten, Michael B. '59, '60, '61
Cowley, Jack '26, '27, '28
Craig, John J. '29, '30, '31
Crain, Jack '39, '40, '41
Crane, Ed '03, '05
Crawford, Charles '69
Crawford, W. J. (Mgr.) '93
Creswell, Frank '96
Cromeens, Mike '73
Crosby, Hugh A. '62, '63
Crosslin, Don '71, '72, '73
Crow, Franklin J. '44
Culp, Yancy '22
Culpepper, John P. '60, '61, '62
Cumley, Steve '73
Cunningham, Don W. '49, '50, '51
Currie, Thomas T., Jr. '63, '64
Currin, Fred '72, '73
Curtis, Abb S. '22, '23

"D"

Dabney, Kelso (Mgr.) '37, '38
Dabney, Ward '95
Dahlberg, Greg '71, '72, '73
Dale, William H. '68, '69, '70
Daniel, Chal '39, '40, '41
Daniel, M. E. '13
Davis, E. Gilmore '38, '39
Davis, Gates A. (Mgr.) '31
Davis, June '49, '50, '51
Davis, Melvin D. '66
Davis, Rick '71, '72
Dawkins, Doug R. '52
Dawson, Gilbert H. '50, '51, '52

Dawson, Ted R. '38, '39, '40
Day, Adison P. '93, '94
Dayvault, Frank '23, '24
Dealey, E. M. (Ted) '12
Dean, Mike '72, '73
Dean, Michael P. E. '68, '69, '70
Debenport, Jerry W. '96
DeLesdernier, John '00
Del Hommee, Louis R. '55, '56, '57
Dell, W. A. '29, '30, '31
Denmark, Andrew W. '95, '96, '97
Dennis, Tom '19, '20, '21
Denton, W. R. '95
Derrick, Leslie '65, '66
Dillon, Bobby D. '49, '50, '51
Dittmar, Gustave C. '13, '14, '15, '16
Dixon, Joe M. '62, '63, '64
Doenges, Joseph H. (Mgr.) '67
Doerr, Timothy M. '62, '63, '64
Doke, Maurice '57, '58, '59
Dolan, Harry '16
Dollar, Charles R. '54
Domingues, Francis J. '20, '21
Doss, Noble W. '39, '40, '41
Dowdle, Don M. '57, '58, '59
Dowdy, Ray '70, '71
Downs, Thomas H. '11
Dreymala, Clarence F. '56, '58, '59
DuBose, William '30, '31, '32
Duncan, Addison B. '15
Duncan, Bowie '05, '06, '07, '08
Duncan, I. V. '00, '01, '02
Dyer, Ben '06, '07, '08, '09
Dyer, Glen C. '54

"E"

Ealey, Donald '71, '72
Earle, H. Sears '32
Easter, John F. '02
Eckhardt, O. G. '22, '23
Edge, Robert L., Jr. '44
Edmond, J. A. '13, '14, '15
Edwards, Fred A. '64, '65, '66
Ehrig, Kenneth D. '68, '69
Ehrig, Ronald L. '65, '67, '68
Eidman, Kraft (Mgr.) '32
Elam, Kyle C. '20, '21
Elkins, Wilson H. '29, '30, '31
Elliott, Darrell J. '64, '65, '66
Ellis, Joe F. '20
Ellis, Joe H. '18
Ellsworth, Ralph I. '43, '45, '46
Emerson, Gover C. (Ox) '29, '30
English, Doug '72, '73
Ermel, William F. (Mgr.) '62
Ernst, Fred A. '54, '56
Estes, John C. '25, '26, '27
Estill, Joe J. '08, '10
Esunas, Bernard J. '36, '37, '38
Evans, Roger H. '44, '46

"F"

Fagan, Ronald '31, '32, '33
Falk, Bibb A. '18, '19
Fambrough, Don P. '42
Faulkner, Staley '61, '62, '63
Feldhale, L. H. '06, '07, '08, '09
Felfe, Elmo R. '45
Feller, James P. '68, '69, '70
Fenlaw, Rick '73
Ferguson, Kenneth W. '61, '62, '63
Ferguson, W. Brownlee '18, '19
Fest, Howard '67
Field, Jackie H. '41, '42
Fincher, Donald F. (Mgr.) '58
Fink, Henry '05, '06
Fischer, Harold J. '41, '42, '44
Fisher, Fred (Mgr.) '05
Fisher, Walter W. '95
Flanagan, Preston S. '40, '41
Fleming, Gene B. '51
Fleming, Steve '70, '72
Flinn, Robert F. '53, '54
Fondren, Walter W., III '55, '56, '57
Fontenot, Raymond '69
Ford, Adrian '72
Ford, Lewis '37
Ford, Tommy C. '61, '62, '63
Ford, William B. '26, '27, '28
Forney, William B. '36, '37, '38
Foster, Hubert '24
Francis, W. H. '04, '05
Franklin, R. W. '98 (Mgr.) '99
Frankovic, Nick J. '35
Frazier, A. M. '03
Freeman, Jack L. '39, '41, '42
Fry, Errol D. '47, '48, '49
Fults, James E. '60, '62
Furman, Davil S. '93, '94, '95
Furrh, J. D. '30, '31, '32

"G"

Gallaher, Peter K. '65
Gamblin, Bobby F. '61, '62, '63

Gardere, George P. '22
Garrett, Floyd '31
Garrett, Julian '40, '41
Garrett, Peirson (Mgr.) '12
Gary, W. H. '10
Gaspard, Glen '71, '72, '73
Gathings, W. C. '01
Gatoura, Nick '30
Gaynor, Robert K. '63
Geldert, Doug '73
Gennusa, Ragan D. '66, '67
Genthner, Charles W. '51, '52
Genung, John A. '60, '61, '62
George, Larry R. '55
Georges, Bill '50, '51, '52
Gerling, Francis '44
Germany, William V. '55, '56
Gidney, Kenneth R. '66, '67, '68
Gifford, Estel G. '62
Gilbert, Earl C. '66, '67, '68
Gilbreath, Irvin S. '34, '35, '36
Giles, Barney L. '64, '65, '66
Giles, Bobby '73
Gill, Audrey L. '41, '42, '46
Gill, John E. '38, '39, '40
Gillory, Byron '45, '46, '47, '48
Gilstrap, Howard C. '21, '22, '23
Givens, John L. (Mgr.) '48
Glascock, Ben L. '03, '04
Glenney, Joe, Jr. (Mgr.) '15
Goad, Howard L. '64, '65, '66
Gohmert, William H. '19
Gooch, J. A. (Tiny) '25, '26
Goodman, James H. '13, '14, '15
Goodman, Leon S. '08
Goodman, Roy S. '58
Goodwin, J. W. '39, '40
Gorman, Leon '23
Gott, Carroll D. '59, '60, '61
Graham, George A. '45
Graham, Lawrence M. '52, '55
Graves, E. Ghent '17, '18, '19
Gray, Archie D. '20, '21, '22
Gray, Herbert W. '53, '54, '55
Gray, Jack S. '33, '34
Gray, Lewis '37, '38, '39
Greear, Ralph '32, '33
Green, Charles L. '17
Green, David W. '45
Green, George M. '19, '20
Green, Hix III '62, '63, '64
Greer, J. Bachman '17, '18, '19
Gremmel, Warren W., Jr. '67
Gres, Marcel E. C. (John) '43
Griffin, Harold '34, '35
Groos, Carl F. '97, '98
Grubbs, James R. '39, '40
Guess, Frank I. '46, '47, '48
Guevara, Robert '71
Gunn, Jimmy '69, '70
Gurwitz, Robert E. '58, '59, '60

"H"

Haas, Charley '37
Hadlock, James R. '33, '34, '35
Halbert, Hal A. '14
Halfmann, Mark '73
Halfpenny, John H. (Jack) '44, '45, '46
Hall, William G. (Mgr.) '68
Halm, Kenneth E. '63
Halm, Kleo G. '58, '59

Halsell, Glenn G. '67, '68, '69
Hames, Robert W. '46
Hamilton, Bill '73
Hamilton, Brodie '05, '06
Hamilton, Lawrence E., Jr. '17
Hammonds, Ralph W. '27
Hanger, R. N. K. '16
Hargrove, William P. '28, '29
Harkins, Henry B. '41
Harkins, James P. '66, '67
Harkins, R. L. '39, '40, '41
Harley, James A. '07
Harlow, Kenneth W. '52
Harold, Edgar '10, '11
Harold, Marion '11
Harper, Thomas '65
Harrell, Thomas O. '45
Harris, Henry F. '41, '42, '46
Harris, Philip L. '63, '64, '65
Harris, Richard C. '94
Harris, Richard O. '45, '46, '47, '48
Harrison, Dan J. '02, '03
Hart, James H. '97, '98, '99, '00
Hart, Louis '73
Hart, Maxey '16, '19, '20
Harville, Clyde Hampton, Jr. '43
Harwell, Samuel R. '16, '19
Harwerth, Robert J. '58, '59
Hastings, Charles H. '05, '06
Hatchitt, Joe B. (Mgr.) '03
Hawkins, Clinton E. '54, '55
Hawn, Charles F. '29, '31
Hawthorne, Jesse J., Jr. '40
Heap, Edwin E. '45, '46
Heap, Walter R. '41, '46
Hebert, Bruce '73

Hedick, Bertram '16, '19
Hejl, James E. '61
Helland, H. R. F. '10
Helland, Hans '72
Helms, James C. '64, '65, '66
Henderson, John P. '35
Henderson, Scott A. '68, '69, '70
Henderson, Simon (Mgr.) '54
Hendrickson, Verne U. '04, '05, '06
Hensley, Lewis L. III '63, '64
Hewlett, John T. (Jackie) (Mgr.) '56
Heyer, George H. (Mgr.) '13
Hicks, Stan '70, '71, '72
Higginbotham, James '12
Higgins, Alfred S. '22, '23
Higgins, Clem L. (Ox) '25, '26, '27
Higgins, M. Frank '28
Higgins, Thomas W. '66, '67
Hildebrand, Stephen W. '60
Hill, George P. '18, '19, '20, '21
Hilliard, Bohn E. '32, '33, '34
Hirsch, Joe (Mgr.) '42
Hobbs, Jack W. '56
Hobbs, Paul (Mgr.) '69
Hodges, Hill '30, '31
Hodges, Osborne '32
Hogan, Pat '73
Hogsett, Sam J. '97, '98
Holder, Lewis G. '46, '47, '48
Holman, Charles M. '66
Homan, Robert B. '24, '25
Homer, Arthur P. '96
Hook, Henry L. '44
House, C. Ben '61, '62, '63
House, Julius F. '95, '96

Householder, Fred W. '04, '05
Howe, Jack L., Jr. '63, '64, '65
Howle, Walter N. '30, '31
Hubbard, L. H. '02
Hubbell, Frank A. '33
Hudson, Earl D. '66
Hudson, James C. '62, '63, '64
Huggins, C. '02
Hughes, Bill '35, '36
Hughes, Thomas F. '26, '27, '28
Hulsey, Simeon H. '20
Hume, David (Mgr.) '36
Hume, F. C. (Mgr.) '97
Hunt, G. Drummond (Mgr.) '02
Hurt, Howard R. '49
Hutchings, Mike '69
Hyde, Walter W. '01

"I"

Ingerton, Gillem '34
Ingraham, Hubert H. '51, '52
Ingram, Tommy '73
Isbell, Tommy '73

"J"

Jackson, Glenn '37, '38, '40
Jackson, Howard L. '58, '60
Jackson, John A., Jr. '02
Jackson, Kenneth G. '48, '49, '50
Jackson, Ransom '45
James, John A. '10, '11
James, T. Harris '01
Janda, Mike '70
Jefferies, David W. '66

Jenkins, Jack '97
Jenkins, Hartford '99
Johnson, Gillis A. '15, '16
Johnson, John W. '52, '53
Johnson, Lionell '73
Johnson, Woodrow '41
Johnston, Charles H. '33, '35
Johnston, Wade '72, '73
Jones, Donald L. '53, '54
Jones, E. Hawley '20, '22
Jones, Grover H. '03, '04, '05
Jones, H. Worth '07
Jones, James C. '50, '51, '52
Jones, James S. '95, '96
Jones, Johnny R. '58, '59, '60
Jones, Murray B. '08, '09
Jones, Roy A. II (Mgr.) '63
Jones, Raymond E. '42, '46, '47
Jordan, Louis '11, '12, '13, '14
Jungmichel, Charles H. '47
Jungmichel, Harold N. '40, '41
Jurecka, Hubert '33, '34, '35

"K"

Kane, Bothwell B. '12
Kazen, Anthony (Mgr.) '52
Keasler, Syd '69, '70
Keck, Raymond M. '14
Keel, John (Mgr.) '29
Keel, Tommy '72, '73
Keeling, Raymond '35, '36, '37
Keithley, Gary '70
Kelleher, Arthur J. '10
Keller, Raymond '99
Keller, Victor J. '01
Kelley, Edward A. '46, '47, '48

Kelley, Edward C., Jr. '52, '53, '55
Kelley, Rodney E. '63
Kelley, Thomas L. '94, '97
Kelly, Pat '71, '72, '73
Kelso, Winchester, Jr. '15
Kennard, M. E. '00
Kennon, Garland '55, '56, '57
Kerbey, Joseph C., Jr. (Mgr.) '04
Kilman, William D. '38
Kinder, T. A. '00
Kindley, George C. '04
King, Anthony P. '62, '63, '64
King, Clarence W. '96
King, Harold '47
King, Joe H. '25, '26, '27
King, John T. '35, '36, '37
King, Rufus G. '25, '26, '28
Kirkpatrick, Arnold L. '09, '10, '11
Kishi, James S. '43
Kitchens, Malcolm T. '52, '53
Knight, Robert E. L., Jr. '14
Kniker, James D. '59
Koy, Ernest '30, '31, '32
Koy, Ernest M. '62, '63, '64
Koy, James T. '67, '68, '69
Krahl, Kenneth (Mgr.) '09
Krahl, William F. '06, '07
Kristynik, David C. '59, '60, '61
Kristynik, Marvin C. '63, '64, '65
Kristynik, Paul C. '68, '69
Kubin, Marvin T. '60, '61, '62
Kutner, Malcolm J. '39, '40, '41

"L"

Lackey, Bobby L. '57, '58, '59
Lacy, Leonard C. '62, '63, '64
Lacy, N. N. '07
Ladd, Dennis '71
Lammons, Peter S. '63, '64, '65
Landry, Ronald P. '65, '66
Landry, Thomas W. '47, '48
Landry, Tommy '71, '72, '73
Lang, William A. (Rip) '16
Lansford, Alex J. (Buck) '52, '53, '54
Lansford, James A. '49, '50, '51
Larpenter, Carl J. '56
Laughlin, William R. '59, '60
Launey, Walton S. '35, '36
Laurence, Ray A. '33
Lawson, Wallace D. '36, '37, '38
Layden, John P. '39, '40, '41
Layne, Robert L. '44, '45, '46, '47
Layne, Robert L., Jr. '67, '69
Leach, Robert J. '65
Leahy, James R. '67
Leaks, Roosevelt '72, '73
Leath, James M. '52
Leavell, C. H. '96, '97, '98
Lee, Bobby C. '43, '48, '49
Lee, Monte V. '57, '59, '60
Lee, R. U. '93
Lee, Robert E. '55, '56, '57
Lee, Sherman '72, '73
Lee, Tommy '70, '71, '72
LeFevre, Albert (Mgr.) '93
Leftwich, S. M. '12
Leissner, Ferd F. (Rube) '20, '22
Lenz, Robert '73
Leonard, Harry '08, '09, '11
Leonard, Offie '09, '10, '11

Leslie, S. F. '00, '01
Lester, Danny Kay '68, '69, '70
Levine, Lewis M. '49, '50
Littlefield, Clyde '12, '13, '14, '15
Lobpries, Frederick E. (Fritz) '41, '42
Long, William C. '53, '54
Losack, Joseph P. '56
Lott, Greg L. '65, '66
Lowrey, Richard C. '55
Lowry, Alan '70, '71, '72
Lucas, Thomas R. '60, '61, '62
Luhn, George M. '23
Lumpkin, Forrest E. (Mgr.) '06
Lyles, Lee '72

"M"

Magliolo, Joseph, Jr. '42, '43, '47
Main, William '43
Mainland, Magnus '05, '06
Mankin, Thomas C. '63, '64
Mann, James S. '60
Marley, James B. '22, '23, '24
Maroney, Don H. '54, '56
Marshall, N. J. '01, '02, '03, '04
Marshall, Robert K. '43
Martin, D. H., Jr. '66
Martin, Vernon '40, '41
Mason, Sammie '73
Massey, Carlton '52, '53
Massingill, M. L. '09, '10
Masterson, Neill T. '04
Mastin, Juliun B. '19
Matocha, Bobby R. '58

Matthews, Edwin V. '56, '58
Matthews, James R. '52
Matthews, Kenneth A. '41, '42
Matula, Tommy '70
Mauldin, Richard D. '63, '64
Mauldin, Stan '69, '70, '71
Mauldin, Stanley H. '40, '41, '42
Maurer, Frederick J. '43
Maverick, George V. '02
Maverick, John F. '94, '95
Maverick, Lewis '96
Maxson, John S. '33
Mayes, Carl H. '51
Mayfield, Ray V., Jr. '44
Mayne, Lewis E. '41, '42
Mayne, W. Harry '33
Maytubby, Joseph S. '96
McBrierty, Sam '70
McCall, George S. '43, '46, '47, '48
McCall, Jim L. '00
McCallum, Alvaro Y. '18, '19, '20, '21
McCauley, Jerry J. '45, '46
McClellan, Claud '99
McClendon, J. W. (Mgr.) '96
McCullough, George H. (Hook) '20, '21
McCullough, George W. '19
McCullough, John T. (Pottie) '25, '26, '27
McCutcheon, W. Currie (Mgr.) '08
McDaniel, D. A. '00
McDaniel, Ned '37, '38, '39
McDonald, William E. '51, '52
McFadin, Lewis P. (Bud) '48, '49, '50
McGinnis, William W. '43

McGraw, Donald R. '52, '53, '54
McIngvale, George '70
McKay, Robert C. '68, '69
McKay, Roy D. '41, '42
McKinney, Mack H. '67, '68, '69
McLane, Paul '93
McLane, Ray '93, '94, '95
McLean, Marrs '03, '04
McLean, William P. '93, '94
McMahon, M. M. '98, '99, '00, '01
McMahon, W. E. '00, '01
McMahon, James W. '06
McMurrey, Allen L. '15, '16
McMurry, John W. '53, '54
McRae, A. L. (Mgr.) '94
McWilliams, A. Perry '60, '61, '62
McWilliams, David L. '61, '62, '63
McQuatters, Osco '01
Meadows, Claude W., Jr. '28, '29
Melcancon, Terry '72, '73
Menasco, Don D. '49, '50, '51
Merritt, Kenneth W. '44
Michalson, J. E. '94, '95
Milan, David '73
Milburn, William O. '50, '51
Milik, Thomas '44
Miller, Alfred M. '48, '49
Miller, Don K. '52, '53, '54
Miller, Richard B. '55
Mills, Henry J. '28, '29
Minor, John M. '41, '42
Mitchell, Joe H. '45
Mitchell, Robert B. '68, '69, '70
Minnick, Malcolm '71, '72, '73
Mintermayer, Henry C. '36, '37
Mobley, Thomas M. '26, '28
Moers, Robert '38

Moffett, James R. '59, '60
Monteith, Walter E. '99, '00
Monzingo, Clayton D. '66, '68, '69
Moody, Herschel '30, '31, '32
Moody, James H. (Mgr.) '46
Moon, Howard D. '52, '53, '54
Moore, Arthur '94
Moore, Bart, Jr. '09, '10
Moore, Fred W. '16, '17
Moore, Gary D. '64, '65
Moore, Jim '71, '72, '73
Moore, Joe W. '20, '21, '22
Moore, Murray W. '24, '25, '26
Moore, Victor C. '93, '94, '95
Moore, Weaver '22
Moreland, Keith '73
Moritz, Eldon L. '56
Morries, Glenn W. '42
Morris, Drewry H. '58, '59, '60
Morris, Harold Brett '62
Morrison, James '93
Morrow, John M. '35
Moses, Robert K. '60, '61
Muennink, Jerry A. '57, '58, '59
Murphree, Bob '20
Murray, William O. '11, '12, '13
Myers, Dan A. '56
Myers, John H. '93, '94
Myers, Park L. '37, '38, '39

"N"

Nabors, Rick '69, '70
Naiser, Charles R. '36, '37, '38
Neal, J. W. '46
Neeley, Jeff (Mgr.) '19
Neely, Stanley '37, '39

Neilson, H. H. '14
Nemir, Albert '29
Newell, Matthew M. '23, '24, '25
Newman, Tom R. '18
Newmon, Steve '73
Newton, Samuel G., Jr. '02
Niblo, Grady '11, '13
Niebuhr, Arthur '31, '32, '33
Nixon, J. W. '29
Nobis, Tommy H., Jr. '63, '64, '65
Norwood, Joe D. '68
Nunis, Robert P. '60, '61, '62
Nunn, Robert R. '17
Nunnally, Knox D. '62, '63, '64
Nunnelly, Guy A. '45

"O"

O'Brien, Tillman D. '58
Ochoa, Richard F. '50, '51, '52
O'Connel, Dan '17
O'Keefe, J. A. '95
Oliver, Derrell M. '61
Olivier, Louis M. '34
Oliver, Robert G. '60
Olle, Edwin W. '25, '26
Orgain, Will E. '05
Overshiner, Edward M. '98, '99
Owens, Charles R. '65, '66
Oxley, Steve '70, '71, '72

"P"

Pace, Bennie C. '68
Pace, Jimmy D. '51, '52
Padgett, H. Edward '59, '60, '61
Padgett, John B. '56, '58
Padgett, Pat '73
Page, Claude D. '50, '51
Pakenham, James A. '49
Palmer, Darrell S. '68, '69, '70
Pantermuehl, R. C. '03
Park, Ralph '40, '43
Parker, Joe J. '41, '42, '43
Parker, R. Daniel, Jr. '94, '95, '96, '97
Parkhurst, Arlis R. '56, '57, '58
Parkinson, David P. '52, '53, '54
Parrish, Lucian W. '03, '04, '05, '06
Patman, Robbie '69
Patrick, R. B., Jr. '39
Patterson, Robert J. '42
Patton, J. Desha '22
Peake, H. Stuart '59
Pena, Dave R. '17, '18, '21
Penn, Albert W. '16, '17, '19
Penney, B. O. '24, '25
Pennington, Marshall '33, '34
Perkins, Milton M. '28, '29, '30
Perrin, Michael W. '66, '67, '68
Perry, Rufus, '10, '11
Person, Vernon E. '54, '55
Persons, James T. '09, '10
Peschel, Randal C. '67, '68, '69
Peterson, A. Paul (Mgr.) '55
Peterson, Gerald R. '55
Peterson, Leo J. '36, '37, '38
Peterson, Lester '29, '30
Petrovich, Charles '51, '52, '53
Petrovich, George, Jr. '44, '47, '48
Petty, Donald S. '60
Peveto, Derwood L. '39, '41

Pfannukuche, H. C. '24, '25
Pfeiffer, Otto A. '96, '97
Philipp, Harold M. '62, '63, '64
Phillips, Charles E. '43
Phillips, Eddie '69, '70, '71
Phillips, Harry '27, '28
Phillips, John (Mgr.) '97, '98
Phillips, Rex '33
Phillips, Thomas E. '62
Philp, John W. '93
Pierson, James D. '52
Pinckney, Steve L. (Mgr.) '11
Pitzer, Bill '34, '35, '36
Ploetz, Gregory P. '68, '69, '71
Plyler, Jimmie F. '43, '44, '45
Poage, Raymond C. '60, '61, '62
Polk, Clifford D. '51, '52, '53
Pool, William C. (Mgr.) '40
Porter, Billy D. '50
Porter, Randon '01, '02
Preibisch, Melvin A. '33
Prejean, Joseph C. (Buck) '31, '32, '33
Prendergrast, D. M. '01, '02
Presley, Mike '73
Price, Charles W. '63, '64
Price, Edwin B. '30, '31, '32
Price, Glenn H. '51, '52
Pritchard, Jerry M. '66
Proctor, Ben H. '48, '49, '50
Proctor, Leslie C. '42
Puett, Nelson, Jr. '38, '39, '40
Puett, Nelson, Sr. '11, '12
Pyle, Billy Baxter '47, '48, '49

"Q"

Quinn, Billy '52, '53, '54

"R"

Ragone, Raymond G. '45
Raley, Bobby R. '50, '51, '52
Ralston, Wallace W. '94, '95, '96
Ramirez, Rene J. '57, '58, '59
Ramsdell, Fred '06
Ramsdell, Marshall '09, '10, '11
Ramsdell, Robert L. '05, '06, '07
Ramsey, Otto (Mgr.) '30
Randall, Jim '70, '72
Rather, Roy L. (Mgr.) '07
Raven, Travis R. '46
Read, Cloyd H. '97
Reeder, Hugh S. '50, '51, '52
Rees, F. A. (Nono) '27, '28, '29
Reese, Cornell '73
Reese, H. Connell (Mgr.) '26
Reeves, Edward C. '55
Reinhard, Charles (Mgr.) '25
Reissig, Gary '73
Reynolds, Charles '27
Rhoads, Orval E. '26, '27, '28
Rhodes, William J. '37, '38
Richardson, David L. '68, '69, '70
Richardson, W. H. '93
Riggs, Michael E. '63
Rike, Gary '69
Riviere, Rob '73
Roach, Joe W. '37, '38
Roach, Travis '69, '71, '72
Roberts, Gordon L. '61, '62, '63
Roberts, Walton S. '41, '42
Robertson, Corbin J. '66, '67, '68
Robertson, G. A. (Mgr.) '00
Robertson, Ivan D. '21, '22, '23
Robichau, Paul '69, '70

Robinson, Don (Mogul) '03, '04, '05
Robinson, George S. '53
Robinson, Johnny F. '68, '69
Robinson, Wallace A. '43
Robuck, Michael '66
Rogers, Charles '69
Rohrer, Tommy J. '67
Rose, Alfred '27, '28, '29
Rose, Jimmie R. '59
Rosser, Homer J. '52, '53, '54
Rowan, Joseph R. '47, '48, '49, '50
Rowan, Mike '70, '71, '72
Roy, R. E. L. '93
Ruckman, H. B. '01
Rundell, Bennie '31, '32, '33
Rundell, Clarence '26
Rushing, Jack '70
Russ, Semp '98, '99, '00
Russell, David D. '59, '60, '61
Russell, Joe H. '10, '11
Rutherford, Bill '71, '72, '73

"S"

Sachse, Jack C. '41, '42, '44
Sam, Leopold G. '99, '00
Samuels, Leslie P. '48, '49
Sanders, Orban (Spec) '40, '41
Sands, Morriss '35
Sands, Walter C. (Sandy) '61, '62, '64
Sanger, Philip '33, '34
Saunders, Walter A. (Mgr.) '57
Sauer, George H. '63, '64
Saxon, Mack '25, '26

Saxton, James E., Jr. '59, '60, '61
Scarborough, W. Dallas '03, '04
Schaffner, Fred L. (Mgr.) '33
Schott, Billy '72, '73
Schreiner, Walter E. '96, '97, '98, '99, '00
Schuhardt, V. T. '24
Schulte, Richard C. '57, '58, '59
Schulz, Hollis H. (Mgr.) '28
Schutze, Edbert J. '44
Schwarting, Joseph F. '41, '42
Schriewer, Menan C. '53, '54, '55
Schwartzkopf, Dale E. '45, '46, '47, '48
Scott, John W. '99
Scott, Wallace H., Jr. '41, '42
Seaholm, Julius T. '51, '56, '57
Seals, J. Raymond '31, '32
Seals, John R. '60
Searcy, S. S. '03
Secor, Joe W. '16
Sellers, James E. '11, '12
Sens, Charles L. '16, '21
Settegast, W. Lester '24
Sewell, Harley E. '50, '51, '52
Sewell, Ike '25, '27, '28
Sewell, Thomas E. '94
Sexton, Robert F. '55
Shands, H. J., Jr. (Bubba) '47, '48, '49, '50
Shaw, Christopher A. '56
Shaw, Howard '71, '72
Shearer, R. B. '24, '25
Sheffield, F. M. (Mgr.) '17
Sheldon, Rick '73
Shelley, Dexter '28, '29, '30

Shelton, Earl L. (Mgr.) '41
Sheridan, Ney '34, '35, '36
Shillingburg, James E. '57, '58, '59
Shirley, Barton A. '59
Simcik, Chester L. '53, '54, '55
Simmons, Bob '73
Simmons, Paul A. '13, '15
Simmons, Robert C. '13, '15
Simons, William L. '43
Simpson, Sylvan B. '15
Sisemore, Jerry '70, '71, '72
Skidmore, Fred A. '54
Slaughter, E. Dick (Mgr.) '96
Slaughter, Edward G. '07, '08
Sledge, Jack '22
Slover, Clint L. '24, '26
Small, Clint '34, '35, '36
Small, Edward C. '65, '66, '67
Smalley, Dewey '24
Smartt, Joe '33, '34, '35
Smith, Bill L. '31, '32, '33
Smith, Christopher K. '66
Smith, Clarence '24
Smith, Elvin M., Jr. '55, '56, '57
Smith, Peter T. '17
Smith, Roy R. '94
Smyth, Louie L. '17, '18
Sneed, Langford H. '53, '54, '55
Souders, Thomas E. '66, '67, '68
Sowell, Charles L. '51
Sparks, Jack '30, '31
Speer, Mike '70
Spellman, Richard M. (Mgr.) '67
Spence, Joe '17, '18
Speyrer, Charles W. '68, '69, '70
Spoonts, Leslie '09, '10

Sprague, Mortimer E. '23, '24
Spring, Gilmer R. '51, '52, '53
Stacy, Franklin '22
Stallings, Leslie C. '10
Stafford, Albert H. '30, '31, '32
Stallter, Maurice T. (Rosy) '24, '25, '26
Stanley, Robert F. '65, '66, '67
Stark, H. J. Lutcher (Mgr.) '10
Steakley, Dan '70, '71, '72
Steinmark, Freddie J. '68, '69
Stephens, W. O. (Mgr.) '94
Stephens, Larry C. '57, '58, '59
Sterling, Walter G. (Mgr.) '22
Stieler, E. R. '07, '08, '09
Stockton, Thomas A. '63, '64, '65
Stolhandske, Carl T. '50, '51, '52
Stolhandske, William F. '58
Stone, Barry T. '66
Stone, Raymond S. '48, '49
Stout, Randy '69, '70
Street, James L. '68, '69
Studer, Stanley S. '51
Sullivan, Bill '65
Sweeney, James M. '38, '40, '41
Sweet, Arthur R. '45
Swenson, A. M. G. '18, '20, '21, '22
Swenson, J. R. '02
Swint, Ronald E. '67

"T"

Taylor, James M. (Mgr.) '01
Talbert, Charles D. '61, '62, '63
Talbert, Diron V. '64, '65, '66
Talbert, Don L. '59, '60, '61

Tatom, William C. '44, '45, '47, '48
Tatum, John P. '53, '54, '55
Terrell, John P. '26
Terry, Howard '35, '36, '37
Terwelp, Dan '70
Thayer, David G. '39, '40
Thompson, Fred '24, '25
Thompson, Jere W. (Mgr.) '53
Thompson, Joseph C. (Mgr.) '61
Thompson, John P. (Mgr.) '47
Thompson, Thorlief '24, '25
Thurman, Rick '73
Thweatt, A. S., Jr. '99
Tigner, Herbert G. '26, '27, '28
Tippen, Homer B. '35, '36
Tolar, Patrick M. '53, '54, '55
Tolbert, James W. '33, '35
Tompkins, Ben H. '50
Townsend, F. Byron '49, '50, '51
Townsend, L. J. (Mgr.) '24
Trabue, William M. '16, '17
Trant, W. M. '54, '55, '56
Treadwell, John C. '60, '61, '62
Tresch, Bob '72, '73
Troberman, Rick '69
Truitt, Charles C. '08, '09
Tucker, Robert A. '54, '55
Tullos, Will J. '36, '37
Turner, Charles E. '13, '14, '15
Tyler, Ronnie '70
Tynes, David L. '20, '21, '22, '23
Tyson, Carl '30, '31

"U"

Underwood, Olen U. '62, '63, '64

"V"

Van Zandt, Harris '33, '34, '35
Vasicek, Victor F. '46, '47, '48
Verde, Jake '34
Vickers, John E. '07
Vining, D. Rutledge '28, '29, '30
Vining, Morgan '10
Vowell, Jack C. '20, '21
Vykukal, Eugene L. '48, '49, '50

"W"

Wade, Thomas V. '62, '63
Wainscott, Loyd D. '66, '67, '68
Waits, Homer C. '16, '17
Walker, Bill '71, '72, '73
Walker, F. Bert '14, '15
Walker, F. Edward (Mgr.) '18
Walker, W. P. '08, '09
Wallace, Jack C. '45
Ward, Jay (Mgr.) '66, '67
Ward, Joe H. '21, '22, '23
Ward, William W. (Mgr.) '37
Wash, Wayne R. '55, '56
Watkins, George H. '41, '42
Watson, Grady '20, '21
Watson, James R. '56
Watson, Jimmie L. '44
Watson, Rembert G. '01, '02, '03, '04
Watt, Richard D. '66, '67, '68

Weaver, Lewis E. '29, '30, '31
Webb, Larry '69, '70
Weedon, John D. '39, '46
Weinert, H. H. '05
Weir, Woodrow W. '33, '34, '35
Welch, Jimmy D. '55, '56, '57
Wells, Perry M. '56, '58
West, Jack M. '41, '42
Wetz, Harlan H. '43, '44, '45, '46
Wetzel, Tom M. '33
Wheeler, James S. '98
Wheeler, Nick '35
Whitcomb, Gail (Mgr.) '27
White, Andrew B. '66
White, Bill M. '52, '53
White, Carl '69, '70
Whittier, Julius '70, '71, '72
Wiegand, Forrest R. '67, '68, '69
Wigginton, Donnie '69, '70, '71
Wilbanks, Theron A. '28
Wilcox, Will '73
Wilkerson, Emmett L. '05
Williams, Don '38, '39, '40
Williams, Joel H. '47
Williams, Joseph D. '58
Williams, Paul N. '49, '50, '51
Williams, Steve '70
Williamson, James N. '67, '68, '69
Wilson, Donald W. '55, '56, '57
Wilson, William D. '49, '50, '51
Wimmer, A. L. (Coke) '12, '14
Winter, Joe D. '56
Wolfe, Daniel M. '47, '48, '49
Wolfe, Hugh O. '34, '36, '37
Wolfe, Sam L. '10
Womack, T. A. D. '53, '54, '55
Woodard, Tommy '69, '70, '71

Woodhull, Frost '04, '10, '11, '12
Woodson, Ben J. '54
Wooldridge, W. Birch '97, '98
Workman, Ronnie '72
Worster, Stephen C. '68, '69, '70
Wortham, R. W. '95, '96, '97, '98
Wray, Steve G. '26, '27, '28
Wright, Stuart P. '24, '25
Wuensch, Robert S. '68, '69, '70
Wylie, Carl L. '56
Wyman, Bill '71, '72, '73
Wyman, Wesley L. '55, '56, '57
Wyman, William, Jr. '55, '56, '57

"Y"

Yeoman, Gary '72, '73
York, Tommy E. '60, '61
Young, Christopher S. '68, '69
Youngblood, Estey (Mgr.) '39
Youngblood, Joe B. '53, '54, '55
Younger, Leighton K. '53, '54

"Z"

Zapalac, Jeff '70, '71
Zapalac, Willie F., Jr. '68, '69, '70
Zunker, Lane (Mgr.) '64